Letts
EDUCATIONAL

Study

FOR GCSE AND A LEVEL

SKILLS

MICHAEL MONTGOMERY

First published 1991
Reprinted 1991, 1992

Editorial team
Angela Royal, Andrew Thraves

Design team
Anne Davison, Keith Anderson   John Hawkins

Text: © Michael Montgomery 1991, 1992

Illustrations: Peter McClure, Bee Willey

© BPP (Letts Educational) Ltd
Aldine House,
Aldine Place
142-144 Uxbridge Road
London
W12 8AW

British Library Cataloguing in Publication Data
Montgomery, Michael *1940–*
    Study skills for GCSE & A level.
    1. Study
    I. Title
    371.30281

ISBN 1 85758 017 6

Acknowledgements

The author and publishers would like to thank the following for permission to use copyright material. Every
effort has been made to trace copyright holders and the publishers will gladly receive information enabling
them to rectify any reference or credit in subsequent editions:

pp. 17 and 19 reprinted by permission of Oxford University Press; pp. 18 and 21 Collins English
Dictionaries; pp. 20, 45, 79, 101, 108 and 110 © Times Newspapers Ltd, 1989/90; p 32 reprinted
with permission from Children's Britannica, 3rd edition, volume 6 'How to train your dog'. Copyright 1981
by Encyclopaedia Britannica International Ltd; p 33 *The Financial Times*; pp. 36, 61,63 and 87 BBC
Magazines; pp. 39 and 43 Philip Allan Publishers; p 44 The Bodley Head; p 52 The Bath Archaeological
Trust; p 55 reprinted with permission from Children's Britannica, 3rd edition, volume 15 'Seasons'. Copyright
1981 by Encyclopaedia Britannica International Ltd; pp. 56, 62 and 67 World Publications Ltd; p 59
Phyllis Mahon; p 60 The Publishing Team Ltd; p 65 Thomas Nelson and Sons Ltd; pp. 75, 76 and 78
© Greenpeace UK 1989; p 130 Northern Examining Association; pp. 131 and 133 Welsh Joint
Education Committee; p 131 London East Anglian Group; p 132 The Midland Examining Group

Printed and bound in Great Britain by
WM Print Ltd, Frederick Street, Walsall, West Midlands WS2 9NE. (0922 643008)

Contents

Introduction

The skills taught in this book are essential to any person following a course of study. As well as GCSE and 'A' level students, many others, it is hoped, will benefit from these skills. They are relevant to trainees in the work place, university and college students and anyone who must organize study time, use a library and works of reference, read books, take notes, present written work and revise and sit exams.

It is the aim of the book not simply to list and describe the skills, but to help you **develop** them by providing practice material.

Practices are set at a level to suit most GCSE and equivalent standard students. **Advanced practices** are appropriate for those at a higher level. Whatever your level, always consider doing the **Practices** because they deal with skills of very wide application. Where answers have been given to the exercises in the practice sections, these can be found at the end of each chapter.

Most subjects have some requirements that demand specific skills. For example, writing with empathy in history, and the need for wide experience when learning a modern language. For this reason, a subject-specific skills section on the major subject areas has been included at the end of the book.

This book has been structured so that it can be used and treated as a 'course' by working through the chapters systematically. Alternatively, individual chapters can be studied in any order as needed: cross-references enable you to follow up any important skills covered in an earlier chapter. The provision of an index also enables the book to be used for reference purposes.

I wish to thank many people who have given help and encouragement with the writing of this book: Eileen O'Hare, Philippa Lamb and Tina Campbell at St Mary's School, Shaftesbury; David Webb at Gillingham School; library staff at Shaftesbury School and Shaftesbury Public Library; and the subject advisers: Nigel Andrews, Peter Goddard, John Harris, Ken Haworth, Arthur Nockels and Derek Thomas, who have given valuable and extensive guidance, particularly for the subject sections.

I am very grateful to Fiona Smith and to my daughters Alice, Bridget and Catherine for the ideas and suggestions they, as students, have contributed. I am grateful, too, to the staff of Letts Educational for their very professional support.

Finally I thank my wife, Liz, for typing much of the manuscript and for encouraging me; and Jenny, Heather and Sandra for the typing they did, too.

Chapter 1
Getting down to work

THE PURPOSE OF THIS CHAPTER

This chapter offers you procedures for ensuring that you get all your work done. There is guidance on how to:

- Divide your time between work and leisure
- Make a detailed timetable
- Use 'evening lists'
- Make use of holiday time
- Work efficiently

The first three sections of this chapter apply to term time.

● YOUR TIME

Before you start to study, it is sound practice:

- to work out how to divide your time between work and leisure. This way you will achieve a sensible balance between the two.
- to work out how to divide your time between your various subjects – again, to achieve a balance.

The advantages of planning your work and making a timetable are:

- it is a means of organizing your time and making full use of it, whether for work or leisure.
- you make a commitment to start a particular type of work at a particular time.
- you avoid simply responding to pressure and giving undue time to work set by your most demanding teacher.
- you resist any temptation to give too much time to your favourite subjects.
- you avoid leaving a piece of work to the last minute and not having enough time for it.
- it is a valuable reminder to you of what you have decided to do.
- you gain confidence: coping with your work will seem less daunting when every task has a time set aside for it.

Here is a suggested procedure:

1 Write down, first, the leisure activities that are most important to you, e.g. a sport, some time with friends, watching certain TV programmes, practising a musical instrument.

2 Make a rough plan of your time for one term-time week.

3 Write on this plan the times needed for your most important leisure activities, for lessons and for meal times. An example is given on p. 6. 'A' level students should note that some of the times marked 'lessons' would be in fact private study periods.

	9.00-10.45	11.00-1.00	Lunch	2.00-3.30	3.30-5.00	5.00-6.00	6.00-6.30	6.30-7.30	7.30-9.00	9.00-
Mon	Lessons	Lessons	Lunch	Lessons			Meal	TV		
Tues	Lessons	Lessons	Lunch	Lessons	Sport		Meal	Musical instrument	TV	Reading
Weds	Lessons	Lessons	Lunch	Lessons			Meal			
Thurs	Lessons	Lessons	Lunch	Lessons	Sport		Meal	TV		
Fri	Lessons	Lessons	Lunch	Lessons			Meal	Sport or musical instrument	TV	
Sat	Work to earn money				Sport			See Friends		
Sun				Go out for the afternoon					Reading	

PRACTICE

Enter in this blank timetable your leisure and social activities, lessons and meal times for a typical week during term time.

Now write 'study' in all the spaces that are not assigned already. If there is not enough time for study, cut back on leisure or social activities.

This flow diagram shows the procedure:

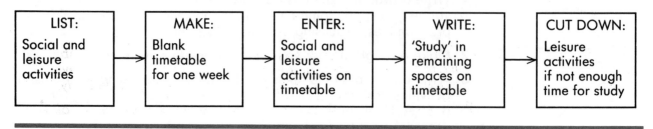

| LIST: Social and leisure activities | → | MAKE: Blank timetable for one week | → | ENTER: Social and leisure activities on timetable | → | WRITE: 'Study' in remaining spaces on timetable | → | CUT DOWN: Leisure activities if not enough time for study |

To make the best use of your time:

- avoid watching more television than you have planned.
- make **full** use of your time. If you have a spare half hour, don't fritter it away. Read a book, start an assignment, **use** the time.
- develop habits. Have roughly the same scheme for each week. If you get used to working at a particular time every Thursday evening, for example, it will come more easily to you to work at that time.
- allow some flexibility in your timetable. If, for example, a friend cancels an arrangement to visit you on a Saturday evening, avoid adopting the attitude that Saturday evening is reserved solely for social activities. Work during that time if it would help you. Spending time studying on that Saturday evening might release time for a leisure activity during the next week.

● MAKING A DETAILED TIMETABLE

The procedure described in this section is one suggested way of ensuring you get all your study done. The next section, on 'evening lists', puts forward an alternative method that you may prefer.

To make a useful timetable, you need to know:

- what study tasks you have to do.
- when each must be completed or handed in.
- how long each task is likely to take.

Break down major assignments (e.g. an English essay, a maths project) into stages and estimate the time needed for each. Here is the breakdown for an English essay on *To Kill a Mockingbird*. Estimate the time needed for each stage in the practice that follows.

> *To Kill a Mockingbird*
> 1. Read Chapters 10-20, make notes.
> 2. Read Chapters 21-31, make notes.
> 3. Study existing notes on Chapters 1-9.
> 4. Read all notes, decide exact title, make essay plan.
> 5. Write first draft of essay.

PRACTICE

1 Enter each of the five English tasks on this timetable at suitable intervals before your deadline, say, Monday at 9 a.m. 'A' level students may use some of the morning times for private study.

2 Choose a major assignment that you have been set and break it down into smaller tasks. List them.

	9.00-10.45	11.00-1.00	Lunch	2.00-3.30	3.30-5.00	5.00-6.00	6.00-6.30	6.30-7.30	7.30-9.00	9.00-
Mon	Lessons	Lessons	Lunch	Lessons		Chemistry homework	Meal	TV		
Tues			Lunch		Sport		Meal	Musical instrument	TV	
Weds			Lunch				Meal		Geography homework	Reading
Thurs			Lunch		Sport		Meal			
Fri			Lunch				Meal	Musical instrument		
Sat	Work in shop			Sport				With friends		
Sun				Family activity/outing						

When you have done work entered on your timetable, tick the entry. As you go through the week, your timetable will accumulate ticks and you will feel encouraged.

Even if you do not keep strictly to your timetable, regard it as a point of reference. It will show you at a glance what work you have to do and the time available for it.

 ● 'EVENING LISTS'

If you think a timetable is unrealistic for you, there is the 'evening list' method.

At the end of each day write down on a piece of paper all the work that you have been asked to do and which you have not yet done. Write down the deadline for each as well. For example, your list on a Monday evening might look like this:

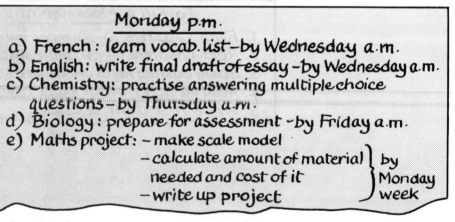

Monday p.m.
a) French : learn vocab. list – by Wednesday a.m.
b) English : write final draft of essay – by Wednesday a.m.
c) Chemistry : practise answering multiple choice questions – by Thursday a.m.
d) Biology : prepare for assessment – by Friday a.m.
e) Maths project : – make scale model
   – calculate amount of material needed and cost of it
   – write up project
   } by Monday week

On Monday evening or Tuesday morning you look at this list and decide what to do first. The pressure is on for French and English (by Wednesday) and you feel you had better make the scale model for your maths project. So you do these three pieces of work on Tuesday. They will therefore drop out of your next work list. But on Tuesday you are given more work to do: in, for instance, geography and physics. So your new list, on Tuesday evening, will look like this:

> ## Tuesday p.m.
>
> a) Chemistry: practise answering multiple choice
>   questions – by Thursday a.m.
> b) Biology: prepare for assessment – by Friday a.m.
> c) Geography: – by Friday a.m.
> d) Maths project: – calculate amount of material ⎤ by
>   needed and cost of it.   ⎬ Monday
>   – write up project   ⎦ week.
> e) Physics: – by Tuesday week.

By arranging pieces of work in order of their deadlines you can see at a glance what work is the most urgent.

PRACTICE

Make a list, of the kind just described, of all the work which you have been asked to do and which you have not yet done.

● HOLIDAY TIME

1 Expect to spend some of your holiday time studying.

2 If you are a GCSE student, it is an excellent opportunity to do a lot of preparatory work for projects and coursework.

3 For 'A' level students it is a good time to catch up on any aspects of your subjects that need extra attention and do any work you have been set.

4 For students at all levels it is a valuable opportunity to read around your subjects to make yourself familiar with backgrounds, historical and wider contexts.

5 For all students it is an opportunity both to revise the previous term's work and to prepare for examinations.

A pleasant aspect of study during the holidays is that you are not under immediate pressure from school and so you are free to spend longer on a topic that interests you or needs extra time. However, do not be lulled into a false sense of security. It is only too easy to let holiday time go by without making the most of it. So follow this advice:

1 Plan how you will use your time. Although you may not construct a very detailed timetable, do use a calendar to work out such things as:
    (a) when you are going away on a holiday
    (b) when you are going to visit a friend or have a friend visit you
    (c) when you are going to work for money
    (d) when you are going to study

2 Do not leave all your study work until the end of the holiday. Complete some of it fairly early on. This will remove any feeling that it is 'hanging over' you.

3 Do some of your study just before the beginning of the next term so that it is fresh in your mind when lessons start again.

Earning money

Many students do part-time work to earn money. Bear these points in mind:

1 Make it a firm rule not to do any work that interferes with your GCSE or 'A' level work. It is **far more** important for you to do

well in these examinations than to have extra money to spend. Families in third world countries often accept a degree of hardship in order to educate their children. You should value education as much as they do and not spoil your chance to get as good a qualification as you can.

2 In term time avoid doing work that will:
  (a) make you feel tired during lessons
  (b) use up time that you need for your study
  A Saturday morning job may be about right. But to do a paper round before lessons would make you tired, as would working late in a restaurant in the evenings.

3 In the holidays there is more time to work for money, but only accept a job after you have planned all your holiday time and decided when you will study.

4 Remember that time spent studying is an investment—in yourself and your future.

● WORK EFFICIENTLY

Getting down to work

The time is 4.30. According to the timetable that **you** have made for **your** work for **your** course it is time to start work. Let us suppose that the task is to read chapters 10—15 of *To Kill a Mockingbird* for your English essay. Do you sit down at once and get on with it? Or do you do one of the following:

  —make a pot of tea
  —read a bit of a magazine
  —chat with your brother or sister a bit longer
  —try on your new jeans
  —look in a paper to see what is on TV tonight
  —take a stroll outside: after all, fresh air is good for the brain?

These actions are simply ways of putting off your work. Recognise them as such; be strong-minded: do not do any of them. Sit down and start work at once. Help yourself by doing the following two things every time that you are about to start work:

1 Take off your watch and put it right in front of you where you can see it all the time. It is a constant reminder that you must get on and do something.

2 Write down on a piece of paper what you are going to do during the next hour. Be realistic, but be specific too. For example, in the case of the English essay, you could write down:
  1. By 5.00 read chapters 10—12 and make notes
  2. By 5.30 read chapters 13—15 and make notes

With this piece of paper and the watch, you have set yourself a challenge. You will get much more done in a given period of time.

Two people work from 4.30 to 5.30. Both sit at their desks for the same one hour. But one does twice as much work as the other. The one who gets only half the work done allowed himself to be distracted, daydreamed and did not set a specific target to achieve during that hour. The efficient worker, on the other hand, looked at her watch and kept an eye on the list of goals and times. Keep going and you will make progress and feel that your time has been well spent. You will feel that you have earned your break.

Private study for 'A' level students

Sixth form students often have periods in the school day which are set aside for their private study. If this applies to you:

- regard these times as opportunities for concentrated hard work. .
- make sure your have all the books, materials, equipment, etc, ready **beforehand** so that you don't waste any of this time.
- find a quiet place for this study, e.g. the library.
- if other students hinder you by making a noise, do something about it. Either reason with them or mention the problem to a teacher. Do not simply allow the interference to continue.

Divide up your work

As stated on p. 7, it helps to divide up the longer pieces of work into stages. Here are two more reasons why this is helpful:

1 A small task like 'read chapters 10–12 and make notes on them' is much less daunting than 'write an English essay'. When you look at the stages, you will see that each is manageable. You will not be put off and so it will be easier for you to get down to work.

2 If you concentrate only on the title on your piece of work, e.g. 'Essay on *To Kill a Mockingbird*', you may think to yourself 'I don't know where to begin'. Once you have written down the stages, this will become clear.

PRACTICE

Stage I: Make a detailed plan of how you propose to spend all your time on one working day in the near future. Include all the work goals you intend to achieve.

Stage II: As you go through that day, make a record on your plan of what you actually did and what work you achieved at each time.

Can you learn anything about your use of time and your work from this practice?

The advice you may have been given about planning your work applies to anyone who has work to do, especially if they work on their own. Here is the plan of a day's work and leisure in holiday time. The student is taking 'A' level history, French and music.

9.00 – 10.30	Read and make notes on Edward IV by C. Ross, pp 1–38
10.30 – 11.00	Break
11.00 – 12.30	Continue Edward IV, pp 39–63
12.30 – 1.00	Break: relax, read magazine/paper
1.00 – 2.00	Lunch
2.00 – 3.30	Practise bass clarinet
3.30 – 5.00	Swimming
5.00 – 6.30	Write first draft of essay on composer Haydn
6.30 – 7.30	Meal
7.30 – 9.00	Watch video of a French film
9.00 – 9.30	TV news
10.00 –	Bed, read novel

If you have a detailed plan for each day, you should get much more done than if you just drift into work.

Chapter 2
Mastering your subjects

THE PURPOSE OF THIS CHAPTER

- To emphasize that your success is your responsibility, but that many people can assist you
- To list some means of achieving success
- To consider the place of learning by heart
- To consider 'using your own words'

 **IT'S IN YOUR HANDS**

Always bear in mind that you are the person who is responsible for your success. Every piece of work you do is for **your** benefit. It is **your** name that will appear on the certificate. If you keep this in mind, then:

- you will not neglect work that you should do.
- you will not be satisfied with work that is below your best.
- you will not relax your efforts, even if you feel that a particular teacher or parent might let you do so.

However, there are people who can give you help and advice.

1 Your **teachers** are allies. They regard your success as their success. Ask them questions during your lessons (don't leave problems unresolved). Alternatively, approach them outside class time if necessary. (See also Chapter 4, p. 24).

2 Your **parents** are there to support you. They can find you a quiet place to study, encourage you, help with your work, help you revise, give advice and share in your successes and difficulties.

3 Your **fellow students** can work with you on some types of assignment; on a project, in practical work, in learning computer skills, or when revising, for example. But, remember to bear these points in mind:
   (a) if cooperating on a project, the work that each student has contributed should be recorded and stated in the project
   (b) if doing practical work, make sure that each of you has a fair share of the 'hands on' experience. No one should monopolize the equipment
   (c) if revising with a partner, avoid wasting time in social chit-chat

Some of the advantages of working with others include:

   (a) it may be more stimulating than working on your own
   (b) each benefits from the other's knowledge, understanding and approach to the subject
   (c) because it is more pleasant, you may be willing to work longer hours than if you were working alone
   (d) discussion generates ideas

4 **Staff** in **public libraries,** museums and archives are excellent sources of information. They can help you in many ways, especially with projects. For further information, see Chapter 4, 'Libraries and other resources', p. 27.

5 Neighbours and **family friends** can often assist in some areas of study. They work in a variety of occupations and usually have valuable knowledge and expertise which they can share with you.

PRACTICE

Choose one major piece of work that you have been recently set (e.g. a project). Consider (i) what help you can reasonably expect from other people with it and (ii) what it is your responsibility to do. Enter each person's contribution on this chart. It is not necessary to do this for every major piece of work. Do it once to discover just how much other people can contribute.

Assignment: ....

My responsibilities	Assistance from other people	
	Person	*Contribution*
....	....	....
....	....	....
....	....	....
....	....	....
....	....	....
Write up work, hand it in	....	....

● HOW TO ACHIEVE YOUR SUCCESS

- organize your time, fitting in all your work and leisure activities. Go back and re-read Chapter 1, p. 5.
- equip yourself with the necessary books, stationery and instruments. If you cannot obtain a book you need, do not give up because someone else is using the library copy. Solve the problem early on. Enlist the help of library staff or a teacher, if necessary. Whatever the situation, remember it is up to you to take the initiative and deal with it.
- make sure that other people do not interfere with the time set aside for your work.
- ensure that you understand your subjects.
- allow no sections in your subjects to go unstudied.
- work carefully and accurately. See Chapter 6, 'Accuracy'.
- ignore boastful friends who get good marks but claim that they do very little work. Do the amount of work that **you** judge necessary.
- revise and prepare for exams thoroughly (see Chapter 14, 'Revision techniques').

Early revision

Revision is strongly associated with exams, but if you also revise throughout your course, soon after you have learnt each topic, then it is a means of **not forgetting** information. Students are sometimes heard to say, for example, 'I learnt that at the beginning of the term, but I've forgotten how to do it now'. Revising throughout will ensure that you avoid this situation.

1 Revise each new topic a week or so after you have learnt it. In Chapter 1 you were advised to make either timetables or 'evening lists' for your work. Look at your **recent** timetables or lists to see what topics to revise.

2 After your first revision, revise a topic again either at the end of the month, at the end of the term or during the holidays.

3 You retain in your memory information that you revise at intervals.

1 List a few topics or assignments you have completed in the last few weeks.

2 Read through them. Check to see if they contain any information, definitions, formulae, procedures, etc, which you need to know but had forgotten. Make a note of these points.

3 Learn the points you had forgotten.

Advantages of this early revision:

- it is quick. This is because everything is still fresh in your mind.
- it is the **best time** to resolve problems. If there is something in your notes you do not understand, you have time to ask your teacher about it.
- it is the **best time** to fill in gaps if you have missed anything through absence from a lesson.
- it will get you **used** to **revising**, so that you will approach revision for mocks or the public examination with confidence.
- when you carry out your final revision, you will not find yourself struggling with topics that you scarcely even understand any longer.

● LEARNING BY HEART

It is not the intention of examinations to make you learn everything by heart. Coursework and examinations are designed to encourage you to reason and think for yourself. This is why so many of the questions provide you with the facts, the data, and then ask you to interpret them, to use your mind and your understanding of the principles of your subject. You are asked to **apply** your knowledge rather than to reel off all the facts you know.

Does this mean that there is no place for learning things by heart? Not necessarily. In many subjects there are some important points which it is useful to learn this way. But it must be said at once that this method is not a substitute for understanding.

These are some types of information you may find useful to learn by heart:

1 Important dates and events (e.g. in history), the main **causes** of a war, the main **results** of it, the **steps** by which a situation arose, the **stages** of a process in biology, and so on. With such pieces of information it is useful to know what **type** they are (methods, causes, etc) and **how many** of them there are.

2 Definitions, especially in science subjects and where there are two easily confused expressions or concepts.

3 Vocabulary or verb parts in a foreign language. How you learn vocabulary in French or Latin, for example, will depend a lot on how you are taught the subject. If your teacher uses the language all the time with you and if you listen to tapes, speak in different contexts and if you read lots of writers in the language, then it may be 'second nature' for you to know the necessary words of the language.

However, it is not always possible for you to encounter language often enough to absorb its vocabulary from its natural context. In this case, you will probably have to learn vocabulary lists by heart:

  (a) learn only a few words at a time. Do this often, if necessary
  (b) learn by testing yourself or have a friend test you
  (c) revise what you have learnt after a few days, otherwise your initial efforts may be wasted

(d) think of the meaning of what you are learning

4 You may also want to learn a few lines of a poem by heart. It may be useful to quote them in an essay, or you may enjoy learning them just because they give you pleasure and you wish to have them always available to you.

5 You may wish to learn a few famous quotations. These, too, may be useful to you in an essay, e.g. 'From each according to his abilities, to each according to his needs', Karl Marx. If you do learn a quotation by heart, learn it exactly, letter by letter and remember who said or wrote it.

However, there are two important points to bear in mind:

1 Be careful about learning by heart the outline or plan of an essay. The question that you are asked in the exam may not match exactly the outline you have learnt, but because you have devoted time to learning it you are tempted to use it anyway. Be flexible!

2 Never learn by heart a whole essay, whether in English or French or in any subject, in the hope that you will be able to produce it in the exam. This will take up an unreasonable amount of your time. The temptation to roll it out at the least excuse may be overwhelming. Some people try to do this out of a sense of insecurity. Gain your confidence by understanding your subject thoroughly.

In conclusion, there **is** a place for learning things by heart. You cannot use your intelligence if you have no facts or data to apply it to. You cannot weigh up and judge events if you don't know what they are. Examination papers often supply you with quite a lot of data, but you need to have a lot of background knowledge of your own in addition to make sense of it.

USING YOUR OWN WORDS

A teacher may say: 'I know this sentence isn't yours. I don't know where it comes from, but I want you to **use your own words**. Do you understand?'

You may well **not** understand. Quite reasonably you may feel that the expert, whose book you have read, expressed the point very well and you can't improve on it. Why write something you think may be inferior?

Teachers and examiners insist that you use your own words because they are interested in the ideas behind the words, not in the words themselves. They want to be sure that the ideas that you write down are ones that you have thought through and not just words you have unthinkingly lifted from somewhere. So if you are writing an essay or project and getting helpful ideas from a book:

- read the text, making sure you understand it.
- look away from it and **out of your head** write down the point in which you are interested.
- if you happen to use a word or two from the original, it doesn't matter because other words, and the structure of the sentence, will be your own.
- if you need to use a particular technical phrase, then look back at your textbook for the expression and get it down correctly.

PRACTICE

The purpose of this exercise is to get you used to thinking of other words for expressing an idea. In the box there are two lists of expressions. Those on the left have been taken from printed texts. Pair them up with expressions on the right which mean nearly the same.

15

an argument is raging	choose goods/articles
forge links with	harmful
tracked down	useful information
select products	household rubbish
interaction	establish relationships with
domestic waste	global warming
detrimental	opposition is increasing
valuable data	traced
targeted on	there is a fierce debate
resistance is mounting	relationship
greenhouse effect	aimed at

Here are two extracts. Extract A is from *Green* magazine. Extract B expresses the same ideas, but using other words. Study them together. Notice how often it is possible to find 'other words'.

Extract A   Since 1983 the 220 000 native people of Sarawak have been struggling against the destruction of their forests by commercial logging companies. An intensive campaign of barricading logging roads has been met by armed police squads and new legislation that means protestors can be gaoled for two years and more.
(From 'Sarawak Scandal', N. Dickinson, *Green* magazine, May 1990)

Extract B   Since 1983, the original inhabitants of Sarawak have been making every effort to prevent timber companies from destroying their forests. When they have systematically blocked forest roads, armed police have stopped them, and there are now new laws so that those who object can be imprisoned for two or more years.

PRACTICE

Now express this text in your own words:

The Penan tribe, who historically live a nomadic life style, are especially vulnerable to rights abuse and have been in the fore of the forest conflict. Forcible resettlement has taken place, while sedentary tribes such as the Kelabit have sided with the Penan.

As the forests that sustain them have been destroyed, many native peoples have been obliged to join the logging crews, but the true vested interests are those in authority; even the Sarawak Minister for the Environment, Datuk James Wong, owns one of the largest logging concerns, the Limbang Trading Company.
(From 'Sarawak Scandal', N. Dickinson, *Green* magazine, May 1990)

ANSWERS

Practice on page 15

An argument is raging = there is a fierce debate; forge links with = establish relationships with; tracked down = traced; select products = choose goods/articles; interaction = relationship; domestic waste = household rubbish; detrimental = harmful; valuable data = useful information; targeted on = aimed at; resistance is mounting = opposition is increasing; greenhouse effect = global warming.

Practice from above (a possible answer)

The Penan tribe, who are nomads, are easily deprived of their rights and they have been at the centre of the forest dispute. They have been forcibly resettled. Some tribes that are not nomadic, the Kelabit for instance, have shown solidarity with the Penan.

As the forests they have lived off have been destroyed, many indigenous people have had to take part in the logging work, but the people who really benefit are those in authority. One of the biggest timber companies, the Limbang Trading Company, is owned by Datuk James Wong, the Sarawak Minister for the Environment.

Chapter 3
Use your dictionary

- To show you how to use your dictionary
- To give you practice in using it
- To encourage you to use it whenever helpful

● **GET TO
KNOW YOUR
DICTIONARY**

It is valuable to have the correct terminology to refer to the various elements of a dictionary entry. Here are some terms:

Headword: the word you look up.
Entry: all the information given about the word you look up.
First/second (etc) sense: a word may have several meanings. 'Second sense' means the second meaning listed in the entry.
Derivative: a word formed from the headword. For example, *electrically* is a derivative of *electrical*.

PRACTICE

Write the correct one of these expressions in each of the boxes below:

derivative entry second sense adjective headword verb definition

intent /in'tent/ 1 *n.* intention, purpose (*with intent to defraud*). 2 *a.* resolved or bent (*on*); attentively occupied (*on*); earnest, eager (*intent gaze*). 3 **to all intents and purposes** virtually, practically. [F or L (INTEND)]

intention /in'tenʃ(ə)n/ *n.* thing intended; ultimate aim or purpose; intending (*done without intention.* [F f. L (INTEND)]

intentional *a.* done on purpose; **intentionally** *adv.* [F or med.L (prec.)]

inter /in't3:/ *v.t.* (-rr-) place (corpse etc.) in earth or tomb, bury. (F f. Rmc (L *terra* earth)]

inter- *prefix* between, among, mutually, reciprocally, [F or L (*inter* between, among)]

interact /intər'ækt/ *v.i.* act on each other; **interaction** *n.*; **interactive** *a.*

inter alia (intər 'eiliə/ among other...

(From *The Pocket Oxford Dictionary*, seventh edition)

**ADVANCED
PRACTICE**

Write one of the following expressions in each of the boxes that follow. If necessary, use your dictionary to find their meanings:

**guideword phonetic spelling inflections variant spelling
indication of usage example etymology noun**

1 ⬚

2 ⬚

3 ⬚

4 ⬚

5 ⬚

treacle

6 ⬚

7 ⬚

8 ⬚

travel (¹træv²l) *vb.* **-elling, -elled** *or U.S.* **-eling, -eled.** 1. to go, move, or journey from one place to another. 2. to go, move or journey through or across (an area, region, etc.). 3. to go, move, or cover a distance. 4. to go from place to place as a salesman. 5. (esp. of perishable goods) to withstand a journey. 6. (of a machine or part) to move in a fixed path. 7. *informal.* to move rapidly: *that car certainly travels.* *n.* 8. the act of travelling. 9. (*usually pl.*)a tour or journey: *Mary told us all about her travels.* 10. the distance moved by a mechanical part, such as the stroke of a piston. [Old French *travaillier* to travail] **travel agency** *n.* an agency that arranges flights, hotel accommodation, etc., for travellers. —**travel agent** *n.*

(From *The Collins Pocket Dictionary*, 1989)

A dictionary offers you a wide variety of information. The more familiar you are with the ways in which it does this, the more you will use it.

PRACTICE

Questions about your dictionary:

1 *Does it include a definition of every headword?*

2 *Does it include an example for every sense of a headword?*

3 *Are examples printed in italics? If not, what typeface is used?*

4 *Does your dictionary tell you the parts of speech of headwords?*

5 *Does your dictionary have one or two entries for the word* **firm***? If two, what is the first difference between them that it indicates?*

6 *Look up the word* **faculty***. Your dictionary gives different senses of the word. How does it indicate that a new sense is being given? How many senses of* **faculty** *are listed? Which of these senses does it have in this sentence?*

   'My father's eyesight and memory are weak now, but all his other faculties are excellent.'

7 *If your dictionary indicates parts of speech, list the parts of speech that* **prompt** *can be.*

8 *On what page are abbreviations and symbols listed?*

9 *Does the introduction tell you how to form the plurals of nouns? If so, on what page?*

10 *How does your dictionary indicate that* **spud***, meaning 'potato' is inappropriate in, say, a geography essay?*

Abbreviations and symbols

Not all dictionaries use the same abbreviations and symbols. However, many are very similar.

In each of the boxes that follow write what you think each of the abbreviations or symbols shown stands for.

1 **gas** n. pl. gases or gasses

2 **nefarious** adj. wicked [[L. **nefas** wrong]

3

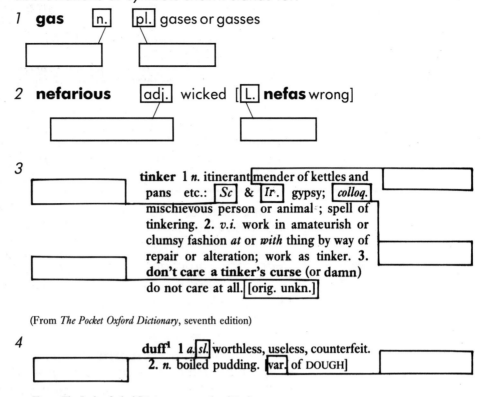

> **tinker** 1 *n.* itinerant mender of kettles and pans etc.: *Sc* & *Ir*. gypsy; *colloq.* mischievous person or animal ; spell of tinkering. 2. *v.i.* work in amateurish or clumsy fashion *at* or *with* thing by way of repair or alteration; work as tinker. 3. **don't care a tinker's curse** (or damn) do not care at all. [orig. unkn.]

(From *The Pocket Oxford Dictionary*, seventh edition)

4

> **duff**¹ 1 *a. sl.* worthless, useless, counterfeit. 2. *n.* boiled pudding. [var. of DOUGH]

(From *The Pocket Oxford Dictionary*, seventh edition)

Look through a few entries in your dictionary. If you see any abbreviations or symbols which you do not understand, refer to the dictionary's list of abbreviations to see what they mean.

● MEANINGS

The two main reasons you refer to a dictionary are:
(a) to find the meaning of a word
(b) to find the spelling of a word

Many words have several meanings. The dictionary lists them, often preceding each new meaning with a number or separating them with semi-colons. When you are reading, how do you know which meaning is correct for a word? Two approaches will help you.

1 Know the part of speech of the word in the context in which it is found. Dictionaries indicate the part of speech before a meaning, so knowing the part of speech will help you decide which meanings to consider. What part of speech is **address** in this sentence:

The conference will address the subject of animal welfare?

You should find the right part of speech first and then look at the meanings.

2 Ultimately, you can only decide between several dictionary meanings after first trying to work out for yourself the meaning from the word's context.

Only try this exercise if you need more familiarity with parts of speech.

1 In which of these sentences is **cross** a noun, a verb, an adjective?
(a) the driver was very cross
(b) do not cross the street now

(c) he wears a gold cross on a chain

2 *In which sentence is **down** a verb, an adverb, a noun, an adjective?*
  (a) the farmer downed his drink in 12 seconds
  (b) I'm feeling a bit down today
  (c) the dog refused to put the bone down
  (d) the field is covered in thistle down

3 *In which sentence is **fast** a verb, a noun, an adjective, an adverb?*
  (a) be careful: those dyes are not fast
  (b) you will have to move fast if you want to buy this car
  (c) Ramadan is a month when Moslems fast
  (d) Lent is a time of Christian fast

This next practice is for reaching meaning through part of speech, context and dictionary.

PRACTICE

1 *Read each extract and answer the questions on it.*

1 More significant for BP are plans to provide North Sea gas to continental Europe, where environmental **concerns** are encouraging governments and consumers alike to substitute gas for coal and oil.
(From *The Sunday Times*, September 9, 1990)

  *(a) In this context is **concerns** a noun or a verb?*
  (b) Is it more likely to mean a feeling of worry, a responsibility (as in 'it's not my concern') or a business ('ICI is an enormous concern')?
  (c) Look in your dictionary to see how the correct meaning is presented.

2 Composite packaging can neither be recycled as metal, paper or plastic. The different **constituents** cannot be separated and they cannot easily be broken down by microbes in a rubbish dump.
(From *Blueprint for a Green Planet*, J. Seymour & H. Girardet, Dorling Kindersley)

  *(a) Which meaning of **constituents** fits this context?*

3 Inside the energy-efficient house, all **implements** are also energy efficient. The fridge and freezer are well-insulated, while the washing machine has a low electricity consumption. The light bulbs are of an energy-efficient design, as is the cooker with its well-insulated oven.
(From *Blueprint for a Green Planet*, J. Seymour & H. Girardet, Dorling Kindersley)

  *(a) Is **implements** here a noun or a verb?*
  (b) What does it mean and what does it actually refer to in this paragraph?

4 Ideally the different water companies would link their distribution networks, enabling those with a surplus to supply those with a shortage. But to **implement** such an ideal state of affairs would be extremely costly.

  *(a) Is **implement** a noun or a verb?*
  (b) What does it mean?

5 In the summer of 1985 six Californians died after eating locally grown water melons. Altogether 1350 people fell ill from the same cause. Hours after eating what looked like perfectly wholesome fruit, they suffered **seizures** and loss of consciousness. Investigators claimed that aldicarb sulphoxide, manufactured by Union Carbide, was responsible.

  *What does **seizures** mean here?*

6 People contemplating certain crimes may be deterred by the threat of the **seizure** of their property if convicted. Poachers stand to forfeit their vehicles, drug traffickers all their assets.

*What does **seizure** mean here?*

2 *Use your dictionary, if necessary, to decide which of the two possible words has the right meaning for the context.*

*1 What **affect/effect** does sulphuric acid have on zinc?*

*2 We arranged to meet the architect at the **site/sight** of the new building.*

*3 My **principal/principle** criticism of the plan is that it will be too expensive.*

*4 Mr McCann is interested in helping drug addicts and so is training to be a **counsellor/councillor** to work among them.*

*5 Having explained the problem, the speaker **preceded/proceeded** to suggest a solution.*

● SPELLING

'I am always amazed when I receive important letters, for example from students applying for university admission, which include spelling errors. Why have they not learnt to check difficult words in a dictionary?'
(Professor Brian Cox, University of Manchester, in *Collins School Dictionary*)

You may simply be **confused** about the right way to spell a word like **aqueous**. If so, look it up!

You may be uncertain how to form the plural of a noun or the past tense of a verb. If so, either look up the word or refer to the grammatical section of your dictionary's introduction.

Be consistent in your spelling:

● use either British spellings or American spellings throughout. Do not combine the two.
● where there are two ways of spelling a word (e.g. realize/realise), make your choice and stick to it.

PRACTICE

Where only some letters of a word are given, work out what the word is and use your dictionary, if necessary, to spell the word correctly. A dash may represent one or two missing letters.

*1 Do blue and white collar workers have **s _ p _ r _ te** canteens here?*

*2 Raw cotton is compressed into **ba _ _ s** and taken to a ginnery.*

*3 The high cost of national defence is a **s _ rce** of great **offen _ e** to many people.*

*4 Jellies of different colours don't necessarily have different **flav _ rs**.*

*5 I **benefi _ ed** greatly from my stay in France.*

Special help

Some people, through no fault of their own, have particular difficulty with spelling. However, there is a reference book that would be found helpful: *The ACE Spelling Dictionary* by David Moseley and Catherine Nicol, published by LDA. The primary arrangement of words in this book is by their **sounds**.

To find the spelling of a word in this book:

(a) turn to a double page index
(b) decide on the first **strong vowel-sound** of the word
(c) decide on the first **consonant-sound** of the word
(d) refer to a grid which leads to a page where the word is listed

If you think this book may help **you**, find a copy in a public library or bookshop to see exactly how it works.

● SOME OTHER USES OF A DICTIONARY

1 To decide whether it is appropriate to use a particular word in a given context. Particularly useful are abbreviations which indicate the following: formal, informal, colloquial, slang, archaic, figurative.

2 To discover the derivation of a word.

PRACTICE

Which of these words have an origin that is Greek, Latin, French or Old English?

criterion	fiddle	matriarch	butter
resolve	catholic	port	stage
pulverize	sympathy		

3 For grammatical information. For example, could you say 'The road was blocked by an accident, so we diverted'? The dictionary puts the abbreviation 'vt' after the word **divert** indicating that it is a transitive verb and needs an object. So the sentence is incorrect and must be rephrased, e.g. 'We were diverted' or 'We had to make a detour'. On the other hand 'vi' after a verb means it is intransitive and does not take a direct object. So, this is an example of just one grammatical point with which your dictionary can help.

4 Most dictionaries tell you how to pronounce a word and where to place the stress. When they use phonetic spelling to do this, a key to it is provided. The **verb** 'transport' may have this phonetic spelling: trænsˈpo:t. The short vertical line tells you the last syllable is stressed. The **noun** has this phonetic spelling: ˈtrænspo:t. What is different in this case?

PRACTICE

Look in your dictionary, if necessary, to find out how these words are pronounced:

elite	homogeneous	panacea	herculean	tetrahedron	oblique
apathy		placebo		counterfeit	septicaemia

The thesaurus

A thesaurus is, literally, a treasure-house of words. It is a rich source of varied ways of expressing ideas. When you use a thesaurus, you find words of similar meaning to the one you look up; you also find opposites. People often refer to a thesaurus when they know there is a good word for what they want to say, but can't remember it at that particular moment. If you are in this situation, look up a word whose meaning is close to the sense you want to express.

Suppose, for example, you want to say that a certain group of people is well-off, but you don't actually want to use 'well-off'. Look it up, all the same. This is the entry in *Chambers Thesaurus*:

> **Well-off** *adj.* affluent, comfortable, flourishing, flush, fortunate, in the money, loaded, lucky, moneyed, prosperous, rich, successful, thriving, warm, wealthy, well-heeled, well-to-do.
> *antonym* poor.

And this is an extract from *Roget's Thesaurus*:

adj. rich, fat, fertile 164 adj. *productive*; luxurious, upholstered, plush, plushy, ritzy, slap-up; diamond-studded 875 adj. *ostentatious*; wealthy, blest with this world's goods, opulent, affluent 730 adj. *prosperous*; well-off, well-to-do, warm, well-feathered, over-paid 375 adj. *comfortable*.

moneyed, monied, worth a lot, made of money; high income, millionaire; in funds, in cash, in credit, on the right side; tinny, well-heeled, flush, credit-worthy, solvent.

Let us suppose that you want to convey the idea that people are making a lot of money and have not just inherited it. Look through the possible expressions above. Perhaps the right word will be obvious to you the moment you see it. Maybe it is 'prosperous.' However, you may not be so certain. Perhaps you only **think** that a word **might** be suitable, e.g. 'flush', 'loaded'. If so, check the meanings of such words in a dictionary and you will avoid choosing inappropriate ones.

Another use of a thesaurus is to find an elegant alternative to a word you have already used once or twice. In the preceding paragraph 'the right word', 'suitable' and 'inappropriate' have been used: different expressions with related meanings.

A thing to avoid is using a thesaurus just to find a more impressive word, because such attempts can lead to errors. One student, for example, who had used his thesaurus for this purpose, read out the short story he had written to the rest of the class and ended with the words: 'That is the abolition of my story'!

Bilingual dictionaries

For details of these see the section on 'Learning a modern language', p. 155.

ANSWERS	
Practice on page 17:	1 entry 2 second sense 3 headword 4 derivative 5 definition 6 verb 7 adjective
Advanced practice on page 17:	1 phonetic spelling 2 variant spelling 3 example 4 noun 5 guideword 6 inflections 7 indication of usage 8 etymology
Practice on page 19:	1 Noun, Plural 2 Adjective, Latin 3 Scottish, Irish, Colloquial, Origin unknown 4 Slang, Variant
Practice on page 19:	1(a) Adjective (b) Verb (c) Noun 2(a) Verb (b) Adjective (c) Adverb (d) Noun 3(a) Adjective (b) Adverb (c) Verb (d) Noun
Practice 1 on page 20:	1(a) Noun (b) Worry 2 'A part of a whole' 3(a) Noun (b) A tool, appliance; electrical appliances like fridges 4(a) Verb (b) To put into practice, carry out 5 Sudden attack of an illness 6 Confiscation
Practice 2 on page 21:	1 Effect 2 Site 3 Principal 4 Counsellor 5 Proceeded
Practice on page 21:	1 Separate 2 Bales 3 Source, offence 4 Flavours 5 Benefited

Chapter 4
Libraries and other resources

THE PURPOSE OF THIS CHAPTER

In a nutshell, the whole world around you, the people in it and you yourself are your resources. This chapter identifies these resources and shows you how you can get the best from them.

● **YOUR TEACHERS**

Your teachers are your most comprehensive resource and they are committed to your progress. They are there:

- to give you a lead: to start you thinking, to introduce you to ideas and possibilities, to show you where to make further enquiries.
- to check that a particular piece of work of yours is advancing as it should. Even when a task seems to you to be going well, it is wise to discuss it with your teacher and listen to any guidance.
- to resolve difficulties. You may be unable to understand a point; you may reach a stage in your work and not know how to continue with it. If so, go to your teacher.

● **YOUR PARENTS**

Your parents may have knowledge and access to information which will be useful to you. Discuss your work with them when you feel they may be able to make a contribution.

● **FELLOW STUDENTS**

You can learn from your fellow students, both by discussing specific points and by working with them on assignments and to develop skills. For further aspects of working with other students see Chapter 2, p. 12.

● **OTHER PEOPLE**

Make the most of any contacts you have with adults in any relevant occupation:

- your parents' friends may have specialist knowledge.
- shopkeepers whom you know may be able to help.
- businesses of many kinds are often willing to help. Large companies, in particular, often have educational material which they will send you. British Steel, for example, provides an education service complete with booklets and films.
- organizations such as chambers of commerce, trades unions, The Rotary Club and The Round Table will possibly offer help if asked.

You have nothing to lose by making a polite approach to any organization you think may be useful to you. But remember that if it has a cause to promote, its literature may be biased, so read and dissect it critically.

● **YOURSELF**

Do not forget that you are an important resource yourself. You have far more useful knowledge than you realize. You are a member of a particular community and as such you have insights into the occupations of your relatives and the way of life of your neighbours. You know a lot, in an informal way, about the local economy and you are able to see the town or countryside around your home.

Whenever you travel, you see a different scene: different features in different towns and cities, other uses made of farmland; mountains in one place, flat plains in another. Particularly if you go abroad you will see differences. Search your memory and recall what you have seen and experienced. Think about it and make use of it, where appropriate, in your work.

● LIBRARIES

These include your public library, your school library, polytechnic, university and college libraries. When you need to use a library, do not hesitate to ask a member of the library staff to help you find the information you require.

Go to your school library and nearest public library at the beginning of your course of study and find out all the ways in which they can help you. On your first visit:

- make yourself familiar with the physical layout of the library.
- discover what its main divisions are. For example, find out:
    - where the main stock of books is kept
    - where novels and other works of literature are
    - where the periodicals are; look for both current issues and back numbers (which you may have to ask for)
    - where the reference section is
    - where any special collection of books is
    - if it has a collection of tapes or other recorded material
- learn what system of classification is used (see below).
- identify the catalogues (otherwise called indexes) and learn how to use them.
- inform yourself about the borrowing system:
    - how to borrow
    - how many books you may have out at any one time
    - how long you may have them for
    - if you can extend the time by renewing
    - penalties for late returns

Classification systems

The books of a library are arranged according to a system so that books on one subject are grouped together and so that every book can be fitted into an appropriate place in the library. It is this system that enables you to find a book when you want it, so it is essential to become familiar with the classification system of every library you use.

Many libraries use the *Dewey Decimal System*. Some use the *Library of Congress* or *Bliss Bibliographic Classification*. Whatever system is used, learn its main subject divisions. These are the main subjects of the Dewey system:

0	General Works
100	Philosophy
200	Religion
300	Society
400	Languages
500	Science
600	Technology
700	Arts
800	Literature
900	History

As an example of how a subject can be divided up and how each division can be further subdivided, here are the numbers for science, and within science for chemistry:

Subdivisions of science		Subdivisions of chemistry	
500	Science	540	Chemistry
510	Mathematics	541	Theoretical
520	Astronomy	542	Practical and experimental
530	Physics	543	Analysis
540	Chemistry	544	Qualitative analysis
550	Geology	545	Quantitative analysis
560	Palaeontology	546	Inorganic
570	Biology	547	Organic
580	Botany	548	Crystallography
590	Zoology	549	Mineralogy

Your library may have guides to its classification system, e.g. a poster listing the main subject divisions under a heading like 'Library Pathfinder' or 'Library Codecracker'.

Catalogues

A library may have one or more catalogues. In each case you look up something you know (e.g. the title of a book) and find information you didn't know (e.g. the classification number of the book). This table shows the uses of the main kinds of catalogue.

Catalogue	You look up	You find
Classified catalogue	A classification number	Titles of books which bear that number
Title catalogue	The title of a book	The classification number of the book
Subject index	A subject	Titles of books on that subject and their classification numbers; **or** just the classification number of that subject. You then go to the classified catalogue
Author catalogue	An author's name	Titles of books by that author and their classification numbers

Once you know the classification number of a book or of a subject, you can go straight to the shelves that bear that number and find relevant books.

You may sometimes have difficulty deciding what word to look up in a catalogue. Suppose, for example, you want a book on oil, you may have to look up not **oil**, but a near **synonym** such as **petroleum**, possibly even **hydrocarbons**. If you want a book on coal, you may have to think of what **larger subject** coal may come under, e.g. **fuel** or **mining** and look up one of these words. It may also help to think of whether you are dealing with oil or coal under the heading of geography or chemistry or technology.

PRACTICE

Suppose you have difficulty finding titles of suitable books on the topics listed here. Think of either a near synonym for each topic or a larger subject it may come under.

1	Castles and fortresses	6	Sir Francis Drake
2	Ballet	7	Stage costumes
3	Satellites	8	Statistics
4	Lasers	9	Comets
5	Coasts	10	Tin

If at first you fail to find a subject or title you want or suitable alternatives, do not give up:

- try again to think of other words to look up.
- ask a member of the library staff.
- above all, persist.

It may take time and effort to track down the information you need, but it is surprising how often you will find it in a chapter of a book on a related topic, for example, or in a periodical or encyclopedia (see p. 28).

Public libraries

Public libraries are underused. Even if your branch is small, it has two great assets: staff who are skilled in finding information and willing to find it for you; and access through the library service to information of almost any kind you may need. Your local branch:

- has books on a wide range of subjects. You may refer to them in the library or borrow them.
- is a place where you can study undisturbed.
- provides a wide range of very helpful services.

The services of a public library are many and various. They include:

1 Readers' request service. Your library can obtain books for you from other public libraries. It takes a week or two and is very useful. Use the microfiche catalogue (microscopic photographs of a catalogue which are projected on a screen for viewing). This lists the complete stock of books held in all the public libraries of your library's county. If a title you want is not listed there, you can still obtain it through the library service as long as it is listed in *British Books in Print*. The service will go outside the county for it if necessary.

2 Special collections. Public libraries often have special collections of books on subjects of local importance. For example, many have collections on local history or a literary figure.

3 Photocopying service. Many libraries will photocopy for you, or allow you to photocopy, reference material such as maps and articles in periodicals. If, for example, you were working on a design or technology project and needed information on British Standards, your local public library would ask the county reference library to photocopy the appropriate pages of the relevant publication. They would be sent to your public library for you to borrow or buy at a modest price.

4 Language learning. Many libraries will lend you tapes which you can use to learn a foreign language or reinforce your learning of it at school.

5 Unpublished material. Public libraries often have collections of documents such as diaries, and illustrations of local scenes and life in the form of drawings, photographs, slides, and so on.

6 Census details. These may be available to you through your public library. They are a valuable source of statistics and information on social life and trends today.

REFERENCE BOOKS

You will find encyclopedias and reference books in the reference section of a library. Since they cannot be taken out of the library, they have the advantage that they will always be available for your use.

Go to an encyclopedia when you want to track down a specific piece of information or when you want a quick overall view of a subject. Obviously an encyclopedia does not have the space to go into a subject as thoroughly as your textbooks do, so it is not advisable to regard it as an alternative to your school texts. However, for more information on points briefly mentioned in your textbooks or for material on related topics an encyclopedia is very useful.

Multi-volume encyclopedias often have a separate index. If so, it is essential to consult the index before going to the other volumes.

These are some encyclopedias you may find useful:

The Encyclopaedia Britannica
The World Book
The New Encyclopedia of Science
Purnell's History of the 20th Century
Chambers Encyclopedia

These are some other useful reference books:

The Oxford Companion to English Literature
The New Oxford Companion to Music
The Cambridge Ancient History
The Oxford Companion to French Literature
Chambers Science and Technology Dictionary
Dictionary of National Biography
The Times Atlas of the World
Atlas of the Early Christian Church
The Oxford Classical Dictionary

PERIODICALS AND NEWSPAPERS

Magazines, journals, reviews and other periodicals have the advantage of being up-to-date. Ask library staff for back numbers if you need them. They may be helpful with historical research, particularly back numbers of local papers. Newspapers also give you access to current information and ideas. *The Daily Telegraph*, the *Guardian*, *The Independent* and *The Times* carry detailed and serious material. Very often these papers carry extensive reports on particular topics. They may survey one industry, devote several pages to a particular country, health, an aspect of mathematics or science, etc. Consider the *Financial Times* as a source of information, too. It covers all areas of interest, not just the economy and business. When reading, distinguish between factual reporting and editorial comment. Read both critically. Ask yourself if a news item or feature article reports **all** the relevant facts. Remember that a newspaper article may well be biased.

MUSEUMS AND EVENTS

A visit to a local museum may spark off an interest in a new field. The Railway Museum in York may lead you vividly into the industrial revolution, the development of transport, an aspect of design and technology. A Dorset museum displays the old button-making cottage industry and leads you into social history. The tiny Colne Valley

28

Museum in Yorkshire takes you into a 19th century weaving workshop and cobbler's shop. Britain has a wealth of such museums—a source of inspiration for project and other work.

Exhibitions and agricultural shows are further stimuli and sources of information. You may make contact with specialists in a particular field who may be willing to supply you with further information to help with your studies.

Look out for leaflets and guidebooks. You may find relevant historical accounts or descriptions of modern technical processes that are unobtainable elsewhere.

● VISITS

Go on educational visits when you can. See:
- forts, castles, battlefields.
- great architecture: cathedrals, monasteries, modern buildings.
- civil engineering works: bridges, docks, airports.
- other countries: deepen your knowledge of another culture, appreciate its geography, history, language.
- factories: of scientific and technological interest.

The possibilities are endless. Go with your family, your school, or a fellow student. Further your understanding of your subjects and your enjoyment too.

● COMPUTERS

You may have access to computers in your school, in a public library, in local authority offices or in many other organizations. Computers can:
- provide you with information.
- enable you to access data, e.g. statistical information collected for a project.
- help you to carry out practical tasks in, for example, map drawing (for geography) and design.
- teach you the skills and concepts of a subject through a set of carefully prepared lessons.

A word processor may be useful for writing up your projects, especially for any correcting or redrafting you may have to do. Most programmes now include a spellcheck facility which may be helpful to some students.

● TV, RADIO, VIDEO

Find out in advance if any programmes are to be broadcast which are relevant to topics you are studying. You may be able to record them on audio or video tape. As with newspapers and periodicals, broadcast material is always up-to-date. Foreign language courses are broadcast and these could be a useful reinforcement of work you are already doing at school. If they are broadcast at an inconvenient time, you may be able to ask someone else to record them for you or use a timing device.

Many schools and colleges now have large stocks of educational videos. You may be able to borrow them just as you do library books.

ANSWERS

Practice on page 26
1 Under history or architecture   2 Dance, music, theatre   3 Space, science and technology   4 Physics   5 Either geography (for land forms) or biology (for coastal life)   6 English history   7 Theatre   8 Maths   9 Astronomy
10 Chemistry, technology or industry

Chapter 5
Understanding and memory

THE PURPOSE OF THIS CHAPTER

This chapter covers:

- The importance of understanding
- The value of linking ideas
- The importance of taking an interest in your subjects
- The value of visual images
- Mnemonics

● DON'T PANIC!

'I don't understand.' Don't panic if you don't understand something the first time you meet it (e.g. the mole in chemistry; the Wars of the Roses in history; mode, median and mean in statistics). Some of these things take time to learn thoroughly. You need to see them worked out in several examples or to read more around the topic before you really understand them. So be patient and allow your understanding time to develop.

Sometimes you may feel 'By now I ought to have understood that idea. Other pupils have got it, but it's still not quite clear to me'. In this case, don't be afraid to ask your teacher again. Nearly every teacher is ready to listen to you sympathetically and give you some extra time, possibly after class. It is much worse **not** to ask. Don't pretend that you know when you don't. If it emerges months later that you never did manage to understand that topic or section, it may be harder to deal with at that later stage. And you may also have failed to understand other ideas which depended on your understanding the first one.

● LINKING IDEAS

'I don't understand it, so I'll just learn it by heart.' It is almost impossible to remember complex things that you do not understand. Don't say to yourself 'I don't need to understand that point, I'll just produce it from my memory if I ever need to'.

You will not be able to do this and the reason is this: we remember things by linking them together in our minds. It is this linking process that constitutes understanding.

For example, how are you to remember that some nouns that end in –y add s to form the plural, while others change the –y to –ies? Here are just a few of them:

delay	delays	alloy	alloys	novelty	novelties
boy	boys	bay	bays	company	companies
tray	trays	play	plays	penalty	penalties
way	ways	fly	flies	victory	victories
valley	valleys	berry	berries	casualty	casualties
key	keys	enemy	enemies	tendency	tendencies

You have the choice of learning each plural separately (there are hundreds of them) or of understanding two patterns: that words with a vowel before the –y add –s, that words with a consonant before the

–y change the –y to –ies. So all vowel –y nouns are linked and all consonant –y nouns are linked. It is obvious that **understanding** these **links** greatly reduces the load on your **memory**.

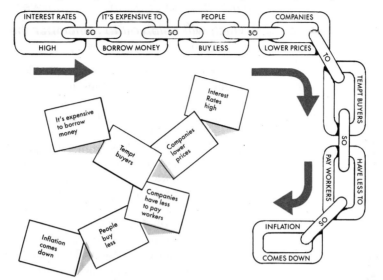

Ideas in your mind form a sort of mental 'net'. Each idea is like a knot in the net and as each knot is linked to the other knots by the threads of the net, so each idea in your mind is linked to other ideas. If you pull one knot of the net (i.e. if you call to mind one idea) other parts of the net (other ideas) come along with it. You remember all the ideas that are tied up with the first one that you have called to mind. But if the ideas are not tied together in your mind, that is, if you do not understand them, then remembering one idea will not help you to remember the others. If you try to remember 20 unrelated points, it will need 20 efforts by your memory. If you try to remember 20 connected points, the memory effort needed will be much less.

PRACTICE

Arrange these points in a sequence starting with number 1. Write 'therefore' between each pair to show that one causes another. 'Cause' is what links them together.

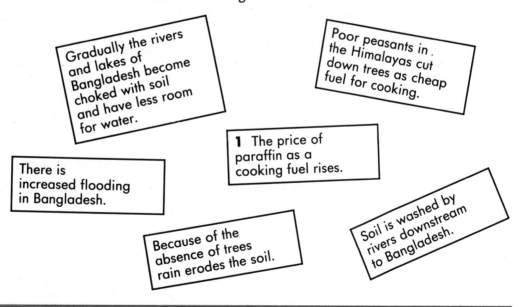

In order to clarify this further, two sets of practice material now follow. First there are two practices. Then there are two advanced practices.

1 *Here is a text on dogs. It is followed by 1 a list of eight of its points and 2 a scheme showing the same information, but with each point clearly linked to the other points.*

Study this material and then answer this question:

Which will help you to remember the information better: the list or the scheme with its links?

It is true that man, in the process of developing the dog to suit his own purposes, has killed almost all the wild instincts and characteristics. He has made it so dependent upon him for food and shelter that without the protection of man the domestic dog is a pretty helpless animal. It is quite unable to look after itself, quite unable to hunt and kill for itself. The wild instincts that would enable it to do so have been lost. There is no more pathetic sight than a stray dog.

However, there are still some traces of the wild ancestor left in the behaviour of the modern domestic dog. Even the most pampered lap dog – the spoilt pet which has never had to do anything for itself and which is descended from many generations of lap dogs that have been similarly pampered over hundreds of years – will turn round and round (and sometimes even scratch the floor) before lying down to sleep. This is an instinct inherited from the original wild ancestor. The wild ancestor did this to make a bed for itself in the earth scratching or forming by the circular movement a small hollow in which to sleep. So strong is the instinct that the modern dog will do it even when it has a comfortable basket in which to sleep. When you see your dog doing this you are watching the wild animal coming to the surface, so to speak, for a moment or two. The wolf, the jackal, and the pariah dog also do this, by the way, so it does not help us to decide which was the ancestor of the dog.

It is the same with bones. Most dogs will bury bones. If a dog is not particularly hungry, it will trot off up the garden with a nice new bone, proceed to bury it (often ruining the best flowerbed) and then forget all about it. The dog forgets all about it because it has no need to remember: man now feeds it regularly. If it does dig it up later on, then it is almost certainly an accident. When the dog was wild this was not so. Then the buried food, we may be sure, was remembered when need arose. Indeed, we know that it was. Wolves in the Arctic, jackals in Africa and India, pariah dogs everywhere, still bury unwanted food and remember where they have buried it and go and dig it up in times of need.

(From *Children's Britannica*, third edition, 1981, vol. 6)

1 List of eight points from the above text:

(i) Man has domesticated the dog.

(ii) Dogs have lost most of their wild instincts.

(iii) Dogs have become dependent on man and are helpless without him.

(iv) Traces of dogs' wild ancestors remain in the domestic dog.

(v) Dogs turn round and round before lying down to sleep.

(vi) Wild dogs made beds for themselves by turning round and round.

(vii) Many dogs still bury bones.

(viii) Wild dogs buried surplus food to find again when needed.

2 Scheme showing the links between the points:

(a) Man has domesticated the dog.

(i) Dog has lost most of its instincts

results

(ii) Dog is dependent on man, helpless without him

(b) but traces of dogs' wild ancestors remain:

Examples *of*
these traces:  (i) *Dogs turn round and round before sleeping*
because wild ancestors did this to make a sleeping place
(ii) *Dogs bury bones*
because wild ancestors buried surplus food to find again when needed

2 *Here is some information about dogs and their noses. To help you remember these points draw up a scheme (or flow chart) showing how they are linked.*

(i) A dog's nose has two important functions:
— the nose keeps the dog cool by the evaporation of moisture from it
— dogs lick their noses to make them wet in order to be cool

(ii) A dog's nose is also used for smelling.

(iii) Smelling is important because a dog gets nine-tenths of its information about the world through its nose.

(iv) The wetter the nose, the clearer the information the dog receives.

(v) When a dog needs to know more about a scent, it licks its nose.

(vi) Smelling was and is important to wild dogs: it told them about the presence of danger and food.

(vii) Domestic dogs lick their noses a lot. This is because the old instinct to do so remains.

ADVANCED PRACTICE

1 *Here is an extract on global warming. It is followed by (a) a list of its nine main points and (b) a scheme showing the same information, but with each point clearly linked to other points.*
Study this material and then answer this question:
Which will help you to remember the information better: the list or the scheme with its links?

All computer models of the Earth's climate predict a warming of several degrees over the next century, if industrial activities continue to change the composition of the atmosphere at the present rate. The biggest single agent of climatic change is carbon dioxide, generated by burning fossil fuels, which traps solar heat in the atmosphere like the glass roof of a greenhouse.

The likely consequences of global warming during the first half of the next century include severe disruption of world agriculture and inundation of low-lying parts of the globe, as the melting polar ice caps raise the level of the oceans.

Although scientists have known for decades that the greenhouse effect is a long-term threat to life on Earth, most climatologists are conscientiously resisting the temptation of saying that it is here already. They maintain that there is still no scientific proof that the warmth of the 1980s is an early sign of man-made climatic change, rather than a natural fluctuation.

The computer models show that we are likely to have to wait another 10 years before the greenhouse effect stands out unequivocally from the natural variations. 'It will probably be around the year 2000 before we can not only say confidently that the greenhouse effect exists but also measure its magnitude', says Professor Tom Wigley of the University of East Anglia's climatology unit.

33

But politicians are beginning to realize that they cannot afford to wait until 'proof' arrives before planning measures to counter the greenhouse effect. So committees to investigate global warming are proliferating. On the international level, an Intergovernmental Panel on Climatic Change is leading the way under United Nations sponsorship.

(From 'A Last Chance for the Atmosphere', C. Cookson, *The Financial Times*, March 6, 1989)

a List of nine main points, 'separate knots':

(i) The Earth will warm if our industrial activity continues.

(ii) Carbon dioxide makes the Earth warm.

(iii) Burning of fossil fuels is the main producer of carbon dioxide.

(iv) Global warming will disrupt agriculture.

(v) Global warming will cause flooding of low-lying land.

(vi) Scientists are not yet certain that global warming is here.

(vii) By 2000 we should know if global warming is a reality.

(viii) Politicians realize they cannot afford to wait until 2000.

(ix) Organizations are being set up to investigate global warming.

b Scheme showing links, 'net':

GLOBAL WARMING

1 Causes and effects

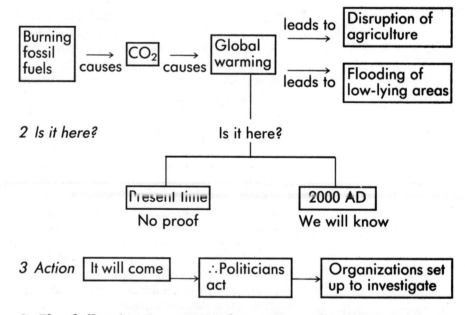

2 Is it here?

3 Action

2 The following is some information about CO_2 emissions. To help you remember these points, make a neat diagram (or flow chart) showing how they are linked.

(i) CO_2 emissions form a blanket around the Earth.

(ii) CO_2 emissions cause global warming.

(iii) Burning of fossil fuels causes CO_2 emissions.

(iv) There are two ways of dealing with the problem of CO_2 emissions.

(v) One method: CO_2 is collected before it is released into the atmosphere.

(vi) This CO_2 is then buried deep in the sea.

(vii) In the other method, the carbon is removed from the fuel before the fuel is burnt.

(viii) The result of this method is that no CO_2 is produced.

(ix) The first method would double the cost of using fuel.

(x) The environmental impact of method one is uncertain.

(xi) Method two would double the cost of using fuel.

(xii) Method two does not leave environmental questions unanswered.

Now you have had a go at all these, make a scheme or flow chart for a topic in one of your subjects.

● TAKE AN INTEREST

People remember things that interest them. If you are very interested in a particular sport, for example, you can remember details of matches, players, their scores, any incidents, etc. If you are not interested in sport, you just will not remember more than a few outstanding facts. If you have a positive attitude to your subjects, it will help you to work and to remember things. If you can become really interested in them, it will help you even more. You can **make** yourself interested in a topic. Involve yourself in it. Try to find out more about a particular point without waiting for your teacher to tell you. The more you throw yourself into a subject, the more interesting you will find it and the easier it will be to remember its details.

● VISUAL HELP

When you studied the scheme on page 32 or page 34 it was hoped that it would help you to remember the information about dogs or global warming by showing you the relationships between the various items of information. It helps you in another way, too. The scheme has a distinctive visual appearance. When you become familiar with it, you will fix its shape in your mind. This shape in turn will help you to retain in your memory the points that go with it. In other words, such schemes and diagrams are valuable memory aids. So use them for this reason, too.

PRACTICE

Read the following extract. Then:

1 Complete the notes on it, giving them a suitable heading. Notice that the relationship of cause and effect is widespread.

2 On the basis of the notes draw a scheme or flow chart to express the relationships between the points. If you like, continue the diagram that follows the notes.

As coastal waters become overfished, larger and more powerful boats are required to enable fishermen to move further out to sea and catch previously unexploited stocks. But as the size of vessels and fleets increases, so fish stocks decrease, and fishermen must then move into still deeper water, giving rise to further demand for new technology and even larger boats.

Locked into this cycle, fishermen are desperate to earn enough money to repay the loans on their boats and equipment – let alone make some kind of profit – and many feel they have little choice but to take every available resource from the ocean, including marine mammals. And as fish stocks decline ever more steeply, so dolphins and porpoises become the most obvious alternatives. In some areas, fishermen resort to using dolphins as bait, because using fish has become too expensive.

(From 'Flipper's Dilemma', K. Mulvaney, *BBC Wildlife*, September 1990)

Notes to complete

.... *(heading)*

1 Coastal waters overfished therefore fishermen go further out

therefore need .... boats

therefore fish stocks ....

therefore ....

2 .... need .... to .... loans on .... and gear

therefore ....

Complete this diagram

.... *(heading)*

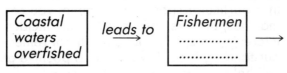

● **MNEMONICS**

These are devices, tricks, for remembering things. They can be very helpful. Here are some examples.

If you find it difficult or confusing to remember that west is 'to the left' of east, just remember that W and E make the word 'we' when they are in the correct position as points of the compass.

This sentence is an example of a popular type of mnemonic: 'Richard Of York Gave Battle In Vain'. The first letter of each word is also the first letter of one of the colours of the rainbow: Red, Orange, Yellow, Green, Blue, Indigo, Violet. If you can remember the sentence, you can work out the colours.

Here is another example: this sentence helps musicians learn the names of the notes on the lines of the treble clef:

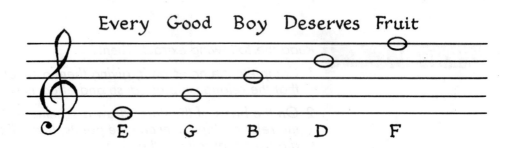

These examples are ready made for you. But most of the time you will have to make up your own mnemonics. A little thought is needed, of course, but it is usually possible. In fact, the very act of trying to think of a way of remembering a set of points forces you to concentrate your attention on them and in so doing helps you to remember them.

PRACTICE

1 *Make up a mnemonic for the notes on the text on overfishing.*

2 *Make up a mnemonic for a set of points you have to remember in one of your subjects.*

Revision is, of course, a vital memory aid. But this is the subject of a chapter of its own. See 'Revision techniques', page 122.

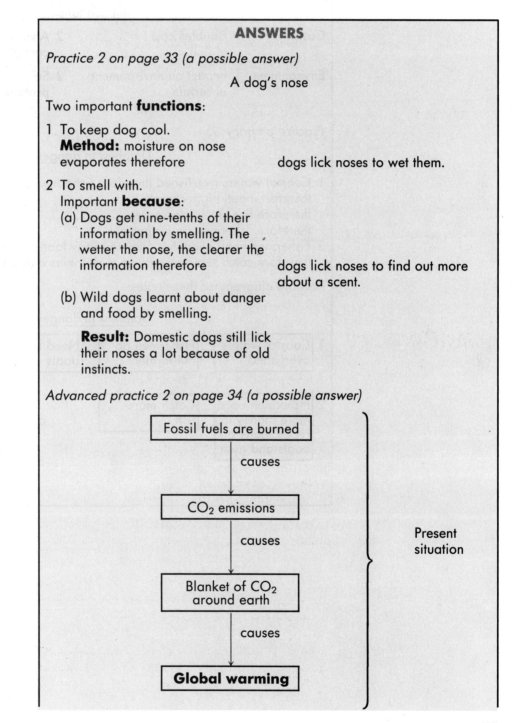

ANSWERS

Practice 2 on page 33 (a possible answer)

A dog's nose

Two important **functions**:

1 To keep dog cool.
   Method: moisture on nose
   evaporates therefore   dogs lick noses to wet them.

2 To smell with.
   Important **because**:
   (a) Dogs get nine-tenths of their
       information by smelling. The
       wetter the nose, the clearer the
       information therefore   dogs lick noses to find out more
                                      about a scent.

   (b) Wild dogs learnt about danger
       and food by smelling.

   Result: Domestic dogs still lick
   their noses a lot because of old
   instincts.

Advanced practice 2 on page 34 (a possible answer)

Fossil fuels are burned

↓ causes

CO_2 emissions

↓ causes

Blanket of CO_2
around earth

↓ causes

Global warming

Present
situation

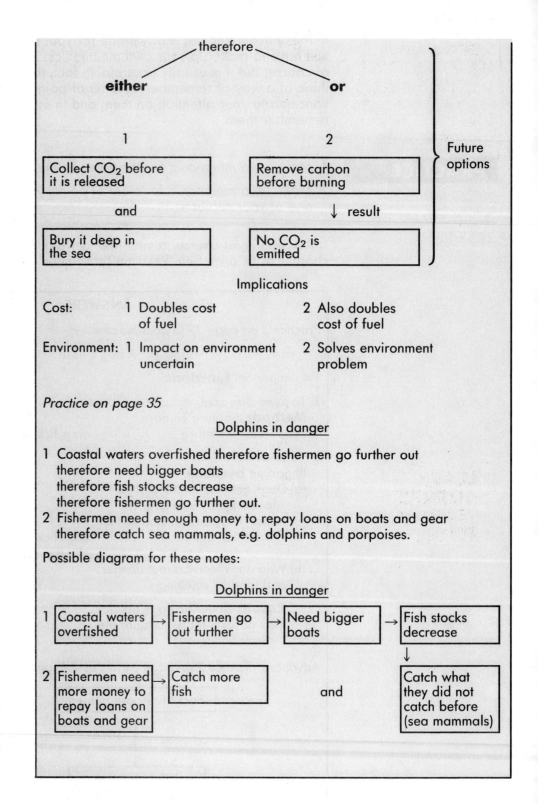

therefore

either   **or**

1   2

| Collect CO$_2$ before it is released | Remove carbon before burning |

and   ↓ result

| Bury it deep in the sea | No CO$_2$ is emitted |

Future options

Implications

Cost: 1 Doubles cost   2 Also doubles
                of fuel   cost of fuel

Environment: 1 Impact on environment 2 Solves environment
                uncertain   problem

Practice on page 35

Dolphins in danger

1 Coastal waters overfished therefore fishermen go further out
   therefore need bigger boats
   therefore fish stocks decrease
   therefore fishermen go further out.
2 Fishermen need enough money to repay loans on boats and gear
   therefore catch sea mammals, e.g. dolphins and porpoises.

Possible diagram for these notes:

Dolphins in danger

1 | Coastal waters overfished | → | Fishermen go out further | → | Need bigger boats | → | Fish stocks decrease |

↓

2 | Fishermen need more money to repay loans on boats and gear | → | Catch more fish | and | Catch what they did not catch before (sea mammals) |

Chapter 6
Accuracy

Accuracy means: (a) being exact and (b) avoiding carelessness. This chapter aims to help you to foster a habit of accuracy by dealing with the following topics:

- The use of technical terms. In order to be exact, it is necessary to distinguish between ideas that are, or appear to be, similar. To make these distinctions clear, there are unambiguous terms to be learned and used
- A critical attitude. Students should be critical of what they read and hear in order to avoid being misled by vague, incomplete or ambiguous statements
- Careful reading. Three specific aspects of language are studied
- Exact expression
- Accuracy in practical work
- Accuracy as an attitude of mind

LEARN CORRECT TECHNICAL TERMS

Correct terminology was woefully rare, with an abundance of terms like 'leaves', 'stem' and 'roots' for **fronds, stipe** and **holdfast** respectively. These did not gain credit.

The vocabulary of genetics was not used with facility; **allele**, for example, was rarely used in place of **gene** where appropriate.

(Both from the Report on the June 1988 Biology A level examinations, Cambridge University Local Examinations Syndicate)

A number of candidates confused **drainage** ditches with **irrigation** ditches.

(From the Report on the June 1988 Geography A/O level examinations, Cambridge University Local Examinations Syndicate)

As you study your subjects:

- be alert to the exact meanings of words.
- notice when a technical term is used in your texts.
- make sure you know exactly what each technical term means.
- distinguish between ideas or words which appear similar or which could be confused.
- revise the meanings of technical terms so that you do not forget them.
- use technical terms correctly whenever appropriate.

PRACTICE

Read this text on acid rain and answer the questions that follow it.

The Nature of 'Acid Rain'

'Acid rain' is the popular shorthand name for a variety of processes which all involve the deposition of acidic gases from the atmosphere. Today the major sources of acidic gases are coal- and oil-burning power stations and motor cars. The principal gases are sulphur dioxide, nitric oxide and nitrogen dioxide. These gases may be deposited directly on surfaces (dry deposition), or become dissolved in water droplets in the atmosphere and be deposited as rain, snow or cloud (wet deposition).

Wet deposition is particularly important in upland areas which are often covered by clouds for long periods. The small droplets which make up the clouds also contain large concentrations of pollutants, generally three – five times greater than those in rain.

Dry deposition predominates in the regions closest to sources of acidic gases, e.g. in towns. Further from the sources wet deposition becomes increasingly important and may predominate in regions of high rainfall such as south west Norway, remote from major pollution sources. In Britain, rain commonly has a mean pH of 4 – 4.5, and this compares with unpolluted rain with a pH of about 5.6.

(From 'Acid Rain', J. Lee, *Biological Sciences Review*, September 1988)

1 *Why is 'acid rain' in quotation marks?*

2 *Is 'acid rain' a technical term? Does it have any shortcomings?*

3 *Does 'acid rain' mean 'acidic gases'? If not, what is the difference?*

4 *Draw a labelled diagram to represent the various ways in which acidic gases are deposited from the atmosphere.*

5 *Which form of wet deposition is most harmful? Say why it is.*

6 *Describe the process of dry deposition from a likely source to a likely destination.*

7 *Is wet deposition a pollutant?*

8 *Name two pollutants.*

9 *Which of the following is a source of acidic gas?*
A Dry deposition   B The motor car   C Nitric oxide   D Water droplets

10 The candidates revealed a very rudimentary knowledge of soil acidity.

(From the Report on the June 1988 Geography A/O level examinations, Cambridge University Local Examinations Syndicate)

*What **is** pH?*

11 *What important distinction between two related ideas is made in this text?*

● BE CRITICAL

This section encourages you:

- not to accept loose statements.
- to ask yourself 'What exactly does this statement mean?'
- to ask 'Is there evidence of this?'
- to look for gaps in arguments.
- to spot contradictions.

If an advertiser claims 'Cats prefer Livermore', do you accept this statement? If so, what are you accepting? You should ask yourself 'What can this claim actually mean?' Does it mean:

– **all** cats prefer Livermore?
– **most** cats prefer Livermore?
– **some** cats prefer Livermore?
– all/most/some cats **always** prefer Livermore?
– all/most/some cats **often** prefer Livermore?
– all/most/some cats always/often prefer Livermore to dry bread?
– all/most/some cats always/often prefer Livermore to 'Megameat'?

and so on.

And on what evidence is the claim based?

1 *Find another advertiser's slogan and see how many interpretations could be placed upon it.*

2 *Read this extract and then answer the questions that follow.*

'Against animal testing,' proclaims a bold black, white and red sign in the front window of The Body Shop, a cosmetics chain that manufactures 'natural' fragrances and skin- and hair-care products. Stacks of promotional literature decry the traditional use of animals to test the safety of cosmetics and exhort the customer to exert your power as a consumer to effect change. Other cosmetics manufacturers are less vocal about the issue, but all are backing away from animal testing.

(From 'Skin stand-ins', *Scientific American*, September 1990)

(a) *Why is **natural** in inverted commas? What problems does the word present? Draw up a list of five natural products. What do they all have in common? What is the criterion for calling a thing 'natural'?*

(b) *What practical action is meant by 'exert your power as a consumer'?*

(c) *What question would you ask the writer about the expression 'backing away from'?*

3 *Answer the question that follows this text:*

EPRI suggests that as much as 55 per cent of electricity used for lighting could be saved through cost-effective means.

Compact fluorescent lamps, for instance, consume 75 to 85 per cent less electricity than do incandescent ones. They typically last four to five times longer than incandescent bulbs. If one balances the higher initial cost of the lamps against the reduction in replacement lamps and installation labour (longer-life bulbs do not need to be changed so often), one can recover the cost of the fluorescent lamps and still save many dollars over the life of each lamp. One can thus make money without even counting the savings in electricity.

(From 'Efficient use of Electricity', A. P. Fickett, C. W. Gollings and A. B. Lovins, *Scientific American*, September 1990)

*One can 'save many dollars' over the life of each lamp. What is missing from the text which would tell us **how many** dollars?*

● **READ CAREFULLY**

Is, may, can, could, etc

Words like these distinguish between fact, possibility, probability, etc. For example, notice the difference between 'There **are** large oil deposits here' (a statement of fact) and 'There **may be** large oil deposits here' (a statement of possibility).

Other words to notice are **might, will, would, should**. Look out for them and interpret them correctly.

1 *Compare these sentences:*

1 *Our new lorry can carry 50 tons.*
2 *Our new lorry could carry 50 tons.*
3 *The new lorry will carry 50 tons.*
4 *The new lorry would carry 50 tons.*

Here are possible implications of these statements. Assign each to the most appropriate sentence:

(a) *if we made some change to it (e.g. altered the design)*

(b) this is its present capacity
(c) if we decided to go ahead and buy it/manufacture it (no decision has yet been made)
(d) this is its future capability

2 *Read this extract and answer the question that follows it.*

A repeat of either the 1857 Los Angeles or the 1906 San Francisco quake, given today's urban sprawl, could be the worst natural calamity ever to strike the United States; it has been estimated that as many as 23 000 people might be killed and as much as $70 billion worth of property destroyed. There is little doubt that the San Andreas will rupture again. The question is, when?

Seeking a useful answer to that question, earth scientists have made the San Andreas Fault one of the most thoroughly instrumented geological features in the world. With strain meters, creepmeters, seismographs, galvanometers, gravimeters, tiltmeters and laser beams they are monitoring, measuring and studying every possible avenue along which a reliable indication of forthcoming catastrophe might appear. The scientists have found a number of ominous signs, but cannot yet be certain what they foretell.

To the north of Los Angeles, in the Palmdale area, instruments have revealed a worrisome change in the earth. Between 1959 and 1975 a 32 000 square-mile area of the surface around Palmdale rose like a soufflé in the oven, bulging upward as much as 18 inches ... . Sophisticated measurements made by space-age laser-beam instruments, satellites and giant radio telescopes focused on a distant quasar are producing data of unprecedented detail and accuracy on plate movement near the fault, but it will be years before scientists have enough of a record to permit conclusions about what is happening, let alone predictions of what will happen.

(From *Earthquake*, B. Walker, Time-Life Books)

Say whether, according to the writer, each of the events listed below:

A *has/have happened*
B *is/are happening, i.e. a continuing situation*
C *may happen – just a possibility*
D *will almost certainly happen*
E *will happen*

Events:
1 *An earthquake in San Francisco in 1906.*
2 *A repeat earthquake along the San Andreas Fault.*
3 *23 000 people die.*
4 *$70 billion worth of property destroyed.*
5 *Instruments set up along the San Andreas Fault.*
6 *The finding of ominous signs.*
7 *Measurements along the San Andreas Fault.*
8 *The rising of the earth's surface around Palmdale.*
9 *Satellite production of detailed data.*
10 *Conclusions by scientists about what is occurring now.*

Qualified statements

Many (candidates) fail to do themselves justice by refusing to take account of all parts of the questions, often by ignoring crucial adverbs and adjectives.

(From the Report on the June 1988 History A level examinations, Cambridge University Local Examinations Syndicate)

Careful reading of the question, picking up phrases like 'in the passage', 'at the end of the novel' 'in lines xx-xx', 'in the last paragraph' directed them (candidates) to the limited amount of material which it was appropriate for them to consider. When they ignored these signals, they often wasted a great deal of time.

(From the Report on the 1989 English Literature Syllabuses A and B GCSE examinations, Northern Examining Association)

Adverbial expressions

Writers often use expressions like **usually, in most cases, to some extent, on the whole, generally** to limit the force or scope of a statement. Expressions like these mean that what the writer is saying does not apply **always** or **in all circumstances**. It is essential to notice this and reflect it accurately in your notes or essays. Here are some examples:

1 Andrew's health has recovered to some extent, but he has had to give up his job.
Question: Is he back to normal health?

2 Damage from acid rain is observed most frequently in old trees.
Question: Are only old trees affected?

3 The small droplets which make up the clouds also contain large concentrations of pollutants, generally three – five times greater than those in rain.

(From 'Acid Rain', see p. 40)

Questions:
 (i) could these concentrations sometimes be only twice as great as those in rain?
 (ii) could they be as much as six times greater sometimes?

Notice adverbial expressions that limit **time** and **place**, e.g:

4 In the early part of the 19th century Loch Enoch had a good reputation as a trout fishery.
(From 'Acid Rain')

5 In the northern hemisphere, because of changes in the use of fuel and in combustion processes, nitrogen oxides have become increasingly important as pollutants.
(From 'Acid Rain')

Clauses with **if** and **when** also limit the meaning of a sentence, e.g:

6 If current trends persist, in about 20 years the developing countries will consume as much energy as the industrialized countries do now.

7 Combustion of fossil fuels, especially coal, accounts for more than 80 per cent of the SO_2 and most of the NO_x injected into the atmosphere by human activity. The nitrogen comes from the fuels and from the air and it combines with oxygen to form NO_x when combustion temperatures are high.
(Both from 'Energy for the Developing World', A. K. N. Reddy and J. Goldenberg, *Scientific American*, September 1990)

Is NO_x always produced when fossil fuels are burnt?

Adjectives

Like adverbs, adjectives often limit the reference of a noun. There are several examples in this text:

Smith was not only the first to describe acid rain; he was also **among the earliest** to describe its **possible** biological effects. . . In Smith's day the **main** cause of acid rain was the extensive burning of coal in the growing industrial towns, but this was not the sole cause. Some industrial processes also created spectacular damage during that period. For example, soda manufacture **by the Le Blanc process** led to the release of large amounts of hydrogen chloride into the atmosphere.
(From 'Acid Rain')

'Among the earliest': Was Smith **the** earliest?
'Possible': Were the biological effects **certain** or **supposed**?
'Main': Therefore not the only cause.
'By the Le Blanc process': Did all soda manufacture lead to the release of large amounts of hydrogen chloride?

For an accurate interpretation it is essential to notice adjectives and adjectival phrases as you read. Here is the comment of an examiner on failure to notice an adjective in an examination question:

Candidates frequently penalized themselves by treating the conservation and loss of heat in a superficial and often inaccurate manner. The question asked for a **full** description.

(From the Report on the June 1988 Biological Sciences A level examinations, Cambridge University Local Examinations Syndicate)

PRACTICE

Read this text about a Viking excavation in York and answer the questions that follow it.

Apart from jewellery, there are several other items commonly worn or carried about. Combs, made from antler or, occasionally, bone, were found in considerable numbers, and were clearly much in use – perhaps not surprising when lice and nits were probably common problems. The combs could be carried in carefully fitting bone comb-cases, some of which had a small hole drilled through them at one end so that they could be attached to a belt or strap by a thong. Most people probably carried a small pocket knife, averaging about 12 cm long, with a wooden or bone handle.

(From *The Viking Dig*, R. Hall, The Bodley Head)

1 Which of these interpretations is most accurate?
A Some of the combs found were made from antler.
B A few of the combs found were made from antler.
C A majority of the combs found were made from antler.
D All the combs found were made from antler.

2 The number of combs found was:
A Tiny B Small C Large D Enormous

3 According to the writer, lice and nits:
A Were not widespread because of all the combs.
B Certainly were a common problem.
C Were certainly a problem, but only a rare one.
D Are likely to have been widespread.

4 How many comb cases had small holes drilled through them at one end?
A All B A few C Most D Some

5 Which interpretation is most accurate?
A It is likely that the majority of people carried a small pocket knife.
B It is likely that a few people carried a small pocket knife.
C It is certain that the majority of people carried a small pocket knife.
D It is likely that everyone carried a small pocket knife.

Precise understanding of words

The quotations that follow show that great care is needed to distinguish, for example, between **suggest** and **show**, between 'x **is** the case' and 'x **appears to be** the case'. Do not report a possibility or a tentative statement as if it were an established fact.

1 Present trends suggest that an increase in greenhouse gases equivalent to a doubling of CO_2 will occur between 2015 and 2050, most likely before 2030.

(From *Global Climate Change*, Dept. of Environment and The Meteorological Office, HMSO)

Do present trends ensure this doubling of CO_2?

2 CO_2 concentration is estimated to have been 280 ppm (parts per million) before the industrial revolution.

(From same source as above)

How certain is the figure of 280 ppm?

3 It appears that the polluted cloud that hangs over Athens consists in winter of the kind of fog that London used to have and in summer of a Los Angeles type smog.

Do you think that analysis of the Athenian cloud has conclusively established what it consists of?

In examinations, too, it is necessary to understand words exactly, as these examiners' comments show:

4 In (a) examples of **countries** were confused with **continents** by some candidates.

(From the Report on the June 1988 Biological Sciences A level examinations, Cambridge University Local Examinations Syndicate)

5 Only the better candidates could distinguish between short-term food aid, emergency solutions and long-term appropriate technology developments such as digging deep tube wells.

(From the Report on the 1989 Geography GCSE examinations, Northern Examining Association)

PRACTICE

Read this text carefully and then answer the questions.

Scientists studying atomospheric pollution are becoming ever more concerned about the appropriately named 'nox' gases.

These are oxides of nitrogen spewed out by cars and industrial boilers. They have recently been linked with a range of health problems, from asthma to cancer, and are also a significant cause of acid rain that has eroded the stonework of Europe's cathedrals and killed lakes and forests in Scotland, Scandinavia and Germany. Nox gases also contribute to city smog by combining with hydrocarbons in the unburnt petrol of exhaust fumes to form low-level ozone. Ozone is protective in the upper atmosphere where it provides a shield against the sun's ultra-violet rays. But at ground level, as an airborne bleaching agent, it can be highly damaging to lung tissue.

A recent report from the American Lung Association said researchers were finding 'new health and ecological damage' in nox, the control of which was the 'key to clean air'. The British Lung Foundation has concluded that nox causes much more severe health problems than sulphur dioxide – the target of most clean-ups at power stations and industrial boilers.

(From 'Innovation Special: Pollution', J. Bird, *The Sunday Times*, September 30, 1990)

1 Does the text state that nox gases cause asthma, cancer and other illnesses?

2 If you got rid of nox gases, would that end acid rain?

3 Is ozone a good thing?

4 'Control' is a word to be wary of. What exactly does it mean in the text?

5 Is sulphur dioxide harmless?

6 Does city smog consist of other constituents besides nox gases?

● EXPRESS YOURSELF ACCURATELY

Examiners often criticize expressions like these:

1 'The spine changes shape'. This phrase is vague. It does not make clear:

- which part of the spine alters.
- in what direction it moves.
- to what degree it changes.

2 'Few people from Scotland visited Corfe Castle (in Dorset) **because it is a long way**.' 'Long way' is not precise enough. The examiners wanted to read that the distance means **additional time** and **additional expense**.

3 'Bad weather'. This is a subjective term. Weather that is bad for one purpose may suit another. It is necessary to qualify the statement and give such information as rainfall and temperature statistics. The Cambridge examiners in their report on the 1988 GCSE biology examination said:

The standard of expression and use of English seemed to be better this year but marks were still lost because the precise meaning of statements was not clear. Weaknesses in spelling were still apparent. Although these can often be ignored, some misspellings lead to the incorrect use of biological or chemical terms, whilst others produce statements which cannot be interpreted. This was particularly important in Question 2 on this paper where it was often impossible to distinguish between the terms **mitosis** and **meiosis**.

Take care to:

- choose the most appropriate word.
- spell it correctly.
- make precise, not vague, statements.

PRACTICE

Choose the expression which is most suited to the context and which expresses the meaning as accurately as possible. Then turn to the answer section.

*1 This soil is not **good/advantageous/all right/suitable** for growing rhododendrons.*

*2 The chest of drawers will not fit in this space. I don't think I measured it **accurately/well/thoroughly/appropriately**.*

3 A: Mr Jones claims he can speak Arabic fluently.
*B: Are you **inferring/stating/implying/disagreeing/denying** that you don't believe him?*

*4 Do you believe in using **pesticides/herbicides/fertilizers/insecticides** to get rid of slugs?*

*5 Although the king was forceful and had a sharp intellect, he suffered from some serious personality **failures/defects/drawbacks/disadvantages**.*

*6 The unauthorized copying and selling of video material robs the **legal/authentic/licit/legitimate/law-abiding/admissible** manufacturers of millions of pounds.*

● ACCURACY IN PRACTICAL WORK

Be accurate:

1 In observations that you make when collecting material for a project. For example, if you use a stopwatch, read it correctly. How many seconds is 1:50 on a digital stopwatch?

2 When recording your observations.

3 When measuring and drawing, e.g. when making a model. When you use a ruler, take great care to position it exactly, allowing for the small gap between the edge of the ruler and the tip of the (sharpened) pencil. Take care also to hold the ruler firmly, with pressure from **above**, so that it does not move while you draw the line.

4 When plotting graphs. Many careless mistakes are made. Do check each point that you plot.

5 When shading diagrams and maps with diagonal lines. Measure the distance between the lines; use a ruler to draw them.

6 When tracing. If labelling a tracing overlay with a photograph, take care to position the labels in precisely the right places.

7 When labelling diagrams and maps. Give titles to drawings and photographs that you include in your coursework.

● ACCURACY: AN ATTITUDE

Accuracy starts from a desire to be thorough and to 'get to the bottom of things'. It is an important academic quality. Obviously, it is necessary to have exact information and data if one is going to reason with the information and base calculations on the data.

Inaccurate people are liable to contradict themselves, say things they don't really mean and lay themselves open to criticism from others. So adopt accuracy as a personal goal in all your academic work: think clearly; understand correctly; express yourself precisely.

ANSWERS

Practice on page 39

1 The quotation marks warn the reader to be cautious about the use or meaning of this expression.

2 'Acid rain' is not a technical term. It is imprecise and could mean dry or wet deposition or both.

3 'Acid rain' is not the same as 'acidic gases'. The gases only become 'rain' if they are deposited directly on surfaces or after being dissolved in water droplets.

4

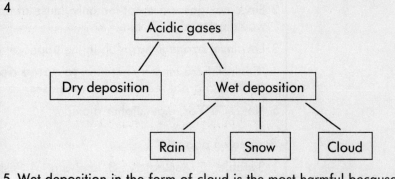

5 Wet deposition in the form of cloud is the most harmful because its concentration of pollutants is three–five times higher than that in rain.

6 A possible answer:

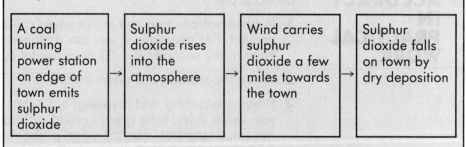

| A coal burning power station on edge of town emits sulphur dioxide | → | Sulphur dioxide rises into the atmosphere | → | Wind carries sulphur dioxide a few miles towards the town | → | Sulphur dioxide falls on town by dry deposition |

7 Wet deposition is not a pollutant. Acidic gases are pollutants. Wet deposition is one **process** by which they are deposited.

8 Two of these: sulphur dioxide, nitric oxide, nitrogen dioxide.   9 B

10 General answer: pH is a scale for expressing the acidity of a solution. A pH of 7 is neutral. A lower figure is acid, a higher one basic.

More advanced answer: **as above and**—the neutral point represents an equal concentration of hydrogen ions and hydroxide ions. The lower the pH figure, the greater the concentration of hydrogen ions, the higher the figure, the greater the concentration of hydroxide ions.

11 The two related ideas are two processes by which acidic gases are deposited on surfaces in the environment. In dry deposition they are deposited directly on surfaces; in wet deposition they are first dissolved in water droplets in the atmosphere and then deposited as rain, snow or cloud.

Practice on page 41

2 (a) The inverted commas warn that 'natural' means different things to different people.   (b) Boycotting the goods.
(c) One would ask 'Are you ceasing **all** animal testing at once?' and 'Are you only using suppliers who have done this already?
3 The missing information is the cost of the compact fluorescent lamps.

Practice 1 on page 41   *Practice 2 on page 42*

1 (b) 2 (a) 3 (d) 4 (c)   1 A 2 D 3 C 4 C 5 A
                               6 A 7 B 8 A 9 B 10 E

Practice on page 45

1 C 2 C 3 D 4 D 5 A

Practice on page 45

1 No. The word 'linked' suggests that the gases may contribute to causing the illnesses.

2 Since nox gases are not the only cause of acid rain, their removal would not end acid rain.

3 Low level ozone is harmful; in the upper atmosphere it is beneficial.

4 'Control' here means limitation **to some degree**. It could mean a small or a great reduction of nox gases.

5 No.   6 Yes, e.g. sulphur dioxide.

Practice on page 46

1 Suitable 2 Accurately 3 Implying 4 Pesticides
5 Defects 6 Legitimate

Chapter 7
Skimming

THE PURPOSE OF THIS CHAPTER

Skimming means discovering in a very short time what topics a text covers. You do this by concentrating your attention on key features of a text, each of which helps you build up a good idea of what topics will follow.

This chapter, therefore, offers three aids to skimming:

- Key features of the text, e.g. chapter titles, topic sentences
- Expressions that signal points in a sequence, e.g. **first**, **another . . . , finally**
- Expressions that refer back to a previous point, e.g. **this problem**

THE RELEVANCE OF SKIMMING

Skimming is the first step in any reading task. It consists of (i) reading the minimum amount of text to (ii) gain the maximum amount of information from it in (iii) the shortest possible time.

Skim a text first if you are looking at it in order to:

- decide whether or not to read it in detail.
- decide which parts of it to read.
- make full notes on it.

KEY FEATURES

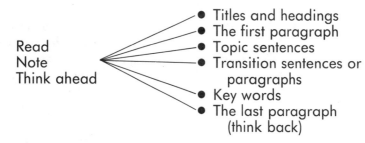

Read
Note
Think ahead

- Titles and headings
- The first paragraph
- Topic sentences
- Transition sentences or paragraphs
- Key words
- The last paragraph (think back)

Use these key features as follows:

- concentrate all your mental energy on them.
- work out what the writer proposes to communicate to you.
- see how ideas in the text are related.
- quickly make mental notes like these:

    'Ah, I expect I'm going to read several **examples** of the previous point.'

    'Now, she's changing the topic from **reasons** for doing x to **methods** of doing x. **Methods** are coming next.'

PRACTICE

1 *Study and complete the analysis of this text by writing the appropriate skimming stage on the dotted lines (if you can't remember these look again at the 'key features' listed above). It may take you a few minutes. But when you have learnt how to skim, you could probably assess the content of this text in about 30 seconds.*

49

Feature	Text	Skimmer's thoughts
Title of book	Viking ships	I will read about Viking ships
Chapter title	Introduction	I will find general points, broad context
First paragraph	In 793 Viking warships descended on the island of Lindisfarne. The Vikings looted the great monastery there, killed some of the monks and carried others off to slavery. This event opened a period of 250 years in which the Vikings dominated the politics of north-west Europe.	This tells me **when** and **where** the Viking warship was important
1 .... sentence	The attack was **shocking** because Lindisfarne was a holy place, known and respected throughout Europe. It was also	I will read about the character of the attack
2 Key .... (*in bold type*)	**terrifying** because everyone had thought that the island was impregnable. That anyone could sail straight across the North Sea to attack it was **incredible**.	I note some key words that confirm this
3 Topic	It was the magnificent ships of the Vikings which enabled them to do the seemingly impossible. These	Now I will read about these **magnificent ships**
4 .... words (*in bold type*)	**ships** were **swift**, **strong**, well built and easily **able** to cross long stretches of open water, no matter how rough. The Anglo-Saxons and their neighbours had ships too, but these were less developed and were mostly used for coastal work or for crossing the English Channel and the narrow seas to Ireland.	5 The key words are about ....

50

6 ....

7 ....
(*in bold type*)

9 ....

Transition sentence
(*looks back and forward*)

In their superb ships the Vikings ranged across almost the whole of the **then-known world**. Danish Vikings attacked **eastern England**, taking their ships far inland along the rivers. Eventually they conquered a large area, including **York**, later known as the Danelaw. Danish Vikings also attacked **France** and under the leadership of the Norwegian Rollo founded the Duchy of **Normandy**. Bjorn Ironside and Hastein even sailed into the **Mediterranean** where they attacked **Spain**, **North Africa** and **Italy**.

To the north, the Norwegian Vikings raided Scotland and settled the Northern and Western Isles. They also ravaged Ireland, founding a number of trading towns including Dublin, and sailed westwards into the Atlantic. They settled first in Iceland, then in Greenland, and from there they sailed to North America where a Viking settlement has been excavated at L'Anse aux Meadows in Newfoundland.

Unlike most of their Danish and Norwegian neighbours, the Swedish Vikings sailed east across the Baltic to the coast of Russia. They sailed up the Russian rivers, and then pulled their boats overland to the rivers flowing south to the Black Sea and the

This paragraph will be about where they went

8 The key words are ....

10 I will read where the .... Vikings went

11 'Unlike' marks a contrast – I will read about a **different** situation: moves in .... direction

51

Caspian Sea. A Viking fleet even attacked the great city of Constantinople.

Last paragraph

Everywhere the Vikings were **after** loot, not only precious objects but slaves as well. They were also **in search of land** to settle, and goods to buy or sell; in fact, anything which could turn a profit. Without their magnificent ships, all this would have been impossible, for it was their ships which unleashed the ferocious energy of the Vikings on the world.

12 'Everywhere'. This pulls the threads together. This paragraph states .... and **how** they raided. Strong emphasis on fine .... Confirms that the topic of this introduction and of the book to follow are (a) the quality of the ships (b) their role for the Vikings

2 *Take one minute to skim the following extract using key features to predict what each section of the text will be about. Then answer the questions that follow it.*

The Roman Baths and Museum at Bath

The Baths

Hot baths were essential to a Roman. At their simplest a suite of baths would comprise an undressing room, a cold plunge bath (*frigidarium*), a bath of tepid heat (*tepidarium*) and a hot bath (*calidarium*) together perhaps with an exercise court. More sophisticated establishments like those at Bath also had a room of intense dry heat (*laconicum*) providing a facility very much like a modern sauna.

After taking exercise the bather would first acclimatize himself to the warm heat of the *tepidarium* before making his way to sit and sweat in the *calidarium*. Here he would be oiled and scraped and possibly massaged before finishing his treatment with a quick plunge in the cold bath.

Bathing was a social occasion where friends could meet and talk, board games could be played and business transacted. There would have been entertainers like jugglers present, manicurists, gamblers calling the odds, as well as hosts of servants and slaves running about looking after their masters. Bathing was a noisy, lively occasion essential to an agreeable life.

Bathing began to become popular in Rome in the first century BC and with it went the need to develop an efficient form of central heating. To heat a room, whether for a hot bath or simply to provide ambient heat for a winter living room, the Romans perfected the *hypocaust* – essentially a cavity floor beneath which hot air circulated. Usually, as at Bath, the floors were supported on stacks of bricks (*pilae*).

The method of heating was by means of a charcoal fuelled flue immediately adjacent to the room and it was quite usual to set a large copper boiler above the flue to provide a constant supply of hot water. To draw the hot air into the under floor chamber it was necessary to create a through draught by means of vertical flues, set in the walls, opening through the roofs. In some cases, when a room needed to be very hot, all the wall surfaces were jacketed with these flue tiles so that no heat would be lost. Sometimes even the vaulted roofs were similarly treated.

The thick masonry of the walls, floors and vaults of these hypocaust rooms ensured that once the temperature had been raised the room would remain hot for a long time – the same principle as the modern night storage heater.

52

The Plumbers
The efficiency of the baths depended to a large extent on the quality of the plumbing . . .

(From text published by the Bath Archaeological Trust)

1 *Look at the headings and the first sentence. What will the text as a whole be about?*

2 *'Suite of baths' is a clue to the topic of the first paragraph. What word is a clue to the topic of the second?*

3 *(a) What will the third paragraph be about?*
(b) What is the first sign of this topic?

4 *What is the function of this sentence: 'Bathing began to become popular in Rome in the first century BC and with it went the need to develop an efficient form of central heating'?*

5 *(a) What will the fifth paragraph be about?*
(b) What is the your first clue to its topic?
(c) If you had to write a few paragraphs on the social aspects of Roman baths, would you continue to read this paragraph?

6 *The extract ends with a heading and the first sentence of a paragraph. What will the next section be about?*

ADVANCED PRACTICE

Take two minutes to skim this text. Then answer the questions that follow it, referring briefly to the text again where necessary.

Title of booklet: **Oil**

Section heading: **Pipelines and tankers**

The crude oil that flows up from a well is of no use to anyone as it is. It must be changed into petrol, fuel oil, lubricating oil, and the many other products that can be manufactured from it. All this takes place in a refinery, but first there is the problem of getting the crude oil there.

It is no small problem, for the movement of oil and oil products is the biggest transport operation ever undertaken. At any given moment, over half the cargo crossing the oceans is oil, and further vast tonnages are flowing through pipelines.

The major traffic in crude oil is from the producing areas to the industrialized nations. In the early days of the industry, crude was usually refined near to where it was produced. Now markets have grown enormously, and the range of oil products has multiplied, and it has become more economic and convenient to refine oil in the countries where oil products are most in demand.

The most convenient way to move oil overland is to pump it along a pipeline. This is basically a long pipe built up from lengths of steel tube welded together. Crude oil pipelines are usually large in diameter, often over a metre across. Pumping stations are built at intervals along the line, so the pipeline can extend over any required distance – hundreds or thousands of kilometres if necessary. The pumps keep the oil moving at between five and seven kilometres an hour.

Laying pipelines is an immense engineering task, especially in remote and rugged areas. They may have to cross mountains, or go beneath rivers, marshes and swamps. Across deserts or other sparsely populated areas the pipelines may sometimes lie on the surface of the land, but in inhabited areas they are always buried.

In many oil-producing regions, pipelines are built to carry crude oil to loading terminals where it is pumped into tankers for transport to refineries overseas. When oil was first transported by sea, it was filled into barrels containing 42 US gallons (35 imperial gallons or 159 litres) – the barrel is still the main measurement used by the oil industry – which were loaded into the holds of ordinary cargo ships. Nearly a hundred years ago, Marcus Samuel, the founder of Shell Transport and Trading, adopted the idea of building ships which were, in effect, floating tanks, and the oil tanker was born.

The main design feature of an oil tanker is the division of the oil carrying space into separate tanks, which prevent excessive movement of the cargo at sea, and enable different types of oil or oil products to be carried. Engines and living quarters are in the after parts of the ship, and so, too, in many modern ships, is the navigating bridge. This arrangement keeps the machinery and accommodation away from the inflammable cargo.

The most striking development in tankers over the years has been a great increase in size and carrying capacity. Per tonne of cargo carried, it is cheaper to build and operate a large tanker than a number of smaller ones. Big tankers also contribute to safety at sea: one 'supertanker' can do the work of up to 20 smaller ships, thus reducing congestion in crowded sea lanes.

Unlike crude oil, natural gas does not need to be refined. After simple treatment, it is ready to use for domestic heating and cooking, as fuel for industry, or as chemical feed-stock.

(From *Oil*, Shell International Petroleum Company Ltd)

1 The first paragraph might lead you to think the text will be about REFINING oil. What key feature BEFORE this first paragraph gives the true topic of the text?

2 What key words in the second paragraph make its topic clear?

3 Can you make a good guess at the topic of the third paragraph from the sentence beginning 'The major traffic in crude oil . . .'?

4 What is your first clue to the topic of the paragraph beginning 'The most convenient . . .' (paragraph four)?

5 Which paragraph reveals its topic in its very first word?

6 (a) Which paragraph deals with the CONSTRUCTION of oil tankers?
(b) Which is the first word that gives a clue of this?
(c) What key words confirm this prediction?

7 What do these key words confirm for you: 'size', 'carrying capacity', 'large tanker', 'big tankers', 'supertanker'?

8 What is the function of this sentence: 'Unlike crude oil, natural gas does not need to be refined.'?

Now you have had a go at practising your skimming skills choose a text that you are expected to read for one of your subjects and skim it quickly to estimate what topics it will cover. Make a note of these predictions.

● **SEEING SEQUENCES OF POINTS**

Writers often present a series of points, e.g. **three advantages**, a **number** of **methods**. It will help you to follow the train of thought in a text if you see the words that signal these points. You could skim a whole page in a few seconds if you saw a series of paragraphs with these beginnings:

The **principal** cause of inflation is . . .
Another important . . .
Thirdly, . . .

Get into the habit of looking out for important signals like those on this signpost:

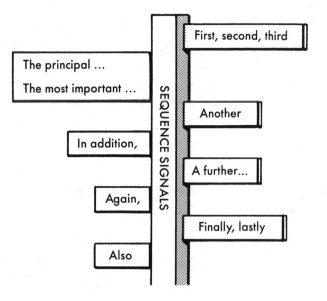

PRACTICE

Read this text; look out for sequence signals and answer the questions that follow it.

Seasonal changes can be observed in the behaviour of living things. One of the best examples is the migration of birds. Punctual almost to the day, certain birds arrive in the temperate countries where they prefer to breed, and then, having raised their young, punctually almost to the day again they depart.

Another example is the instinct to hibernate, or sleep in the winter, which rules the behaviour of some animals. An unusually warm day in winter may cause some of them to wake up, but only for a little while. Not until the season has run its course do they wake up in earnest.

Plants also show seasonal changes. With the coming of spring the sap begins to flow, feeding the waking buds until they blossom into leaf and flower. When autumn comes, the sap reverses its flow and stores the necessary food in the roots to last for the winter's sleep.

The townsman can live almost unaffected by the seasons, merely grumbling when the winter grows too cold and rejoicing over a fine summer for his holiday. To the farmer, however, the seaons are all-important. By them he lives and regulates his calendar and knows when to plough and sow and reap.

(From *Children's Britannica*, third edition 1981, vol. 15)

1 *What phrase signals the first seasonal change that is described?*
2 *What phrase signals the second seasonal change?*
3 *What is the second seasonal change? State it in one word.*
4 *What expression signals the third seasonal change?*
5 *Which sentence expresses the topic of the text as a whole?*

ADVANCED PRACTICE

Read this text. It gives CAUSES that MAKE things happen. Look out for sequence signals and key words. Answer the questions that follow the text.

How the Weather Works

The same forces that form a hurricane also turn showers into sunshine. The processes that shape the weather are at once very simple and impossible to predict with long-term accuracy.

The weather is really a jigsaw puzzle, a jumble of different factors that combine to produce the phenomena we experience as wind, rain and sunshine. Of these pieces, the most important are the sun itself, the Earth and its movement, the oceans and the land masses of the globe. Each of these larger pieces is in turn influenced by smaller ones until one reaches perhaps the most important single factor that influences the weather – the water molecule.

Water vapour absorbs heat which would otherwise radiate back into space. Water also . . .

Another critical factor is the tilt of the Earth. Our planet is inclined at an angle of 23.5 degrees to the plane of its orbit around the sun. This causes variations in sunlight levels which . . .

However, this simple picture is greatly complicated by another important factor – the rotation of the Earth. This causes any free-moving gas or fluid to be deflected to the right in the northern hemisphere . . . .Crucially this effect becomes more intense the closer one gets to the poles . . .

The oceans also play a major role in influencing the weather, acting as vast reservoirs of heat.

(From 'A Jigsaw in the Air', R. McKie, *Observer Special*, April 15, 1990)

1 Which topic sentence tells us to expect a set of causes?

2 What phrase signals discussion of the first cause?

3 What phrase signals the second cause?

4 What expression signals the third cause?

5 What expression signals the fourth cause?

6 'Forces' is a key noun meaning 'causes' in this text. What other noun meaning 'cause' is very common in it?

7 'Turn into' and 'shape' are key verbs with a causal meaning. Quote two others from this text.

● BACK REFERENCES

You read this: ' "My goodness, they were expensive!" ' came the cry from three of my non-organically-minded friends around the country . . . ' and you ask: '**What** were expensive?' because you know that **they** always refers back to people or things previously mentioned – at least, it ought to. In this case the writer has not provided a noun for **they** to refer to. This was done for dramatic effect.

Texts include many expressions that refer back to recently mentioned people, things and ideas. For example:

- pronouns: he, she, it, they, them.
- demonstratives: this, that, these, those.
- demonstratives with nouns: this project, these reasons, this situation, those problems.
- other expressions: there, the other, another, such.

Such expressions are a shorthand way of referring to a previous idea. You, the reader, must make sure you know what these words stand for. When you see 'this situation', for example, you should be able to say to yourself 'Oh yes, the writer means . . . (a situation just described)'.

PRACTICE

Read the following and answer the questions that follow it.

'My goodness, they were expensive!' came the cry from three of my non-organically-minded friends around the country whom I had asked to check out the availability and cost of organic produce in their local supermarkets. And indeed 'organics' are expensive: anything from 20 to 200 per cent more than the standard produce. **These figures** were quoted to me by all the multiples that I spoke to, and borne out by my 'on the ground' researchers. Why **so much more**? Surely it does not cost so much extra to grow a carrot without chemical fertilizers or pesticides?

Well, no, the actual growing does not necessarily cost that much more, but of course **that** is not the whole story . . .

Transport of small quantities, which is all we are currently talking about when we refer to organic produce, packaging of small quantities, distribution of small quantities; all are appreciably more expensive than **the same services** performed in bulk.

Added to **this** is the fact that organic farming has, until now, been carried out mainly by enthusiasts who farmed organically because they believed in organic principles, not by hard-nosed farmers out to make the best commercial job. **This** has meant that in many cases the job has maybe not been done in the most efficient, and therefore cost effective, way.

To their credit, at least two of the multiples are now attempting to remedy **this situation**. Safeways are investing heavily in an organic research farm in Scotland in an attempt to bring organically-farmed produce more in line with what the standard supermarket needs, and Tescos have been working closely with the Soil Association and Organic Farm Foods to improve and streamline packaging and distribution of organic produce.

Even so, as I said to all the multiples that I spoke to, **these problems** are not sufficient to justify a 100 to 150 per cent hike in prices for organic goods. What extra costs are involved? **They** claim that there are two other major factors.

One is availability, and this presents a problem not only in cost terms. Even in Europe the organic market is still relatively small, but it is a great deal more developed than **it** is here, and most European countries already have their sources of supply organized.

(From 'Supermarkets and Organic Foods', M. Berriedale-Johnson, *Environment Now*, March 1990)

1 What does **these figures** refer to?

2 What does **so much more** mean exactly?

3 What does **that** (in the second paragraph) refer to?

4 What services are meant by the expression **the same services** in the third paragraph?

5 What does **this** (fourth paragraph) refer to?

6 Say what each of the other expressions in bold refers to.

7 Read one page in one of your textbooks. Whenever you come across an expression that refers back, make sure you know what it refers to.

Advanced practice on page 53

1 The section heading **Pipelines and tankers**.
2 Key words: 'movement', 'transport', 'cargo crossing', 'flowing'.
3 The topic is likely to be the **direction** of the transport of crude oil.
4 The first clue is 'way'. We are to read about a method of moving oil.
5 Paragraph five. Its first word is 'Laying' and laying pipelines is its topic.
6 (a) Paragraph seven.   (b) 'Design'.
   (c) 'carrying space', 'separate tanks', 'engines', 'living quarters', 'after
       parts', 'navigating bridge', 'machinery', 'accommodation', 'cargo'.
7 They confirm that the paragraph is about the increasing size of oil
   tankers.
8 It is a transition sentence. The topic is changing from the movement of
   crude oil to the movement of natural gas.

Practice on page 55

1 'One of the best examples'.   2 'Another example'.
3 Hibernation.   4 'Also'.
5 The first sentence.

Advanced practice on page 55

1 'The weather is really a giant jigsaw puzzle, a jumble of different
   factors that combine to produce the phenomena we experience as wind,
   rain and sunshine.'
2 'The most important single factor that influences the weather'.
3 'Another critical factor'.   4 'Another important factor'.
5 'Also'.   6 'Factor'.
7 Two of these: 'form', 'produce', 'influence', 'cause'.

Practice on page 56

1 20 to 200 per cent.
2 The phrase means 'as much as 20 to 200 per cent more'.
3 **That** refers to the cost of growing organic produce.
4 **The same services** means transportation, packaging and distribution.
5 **This** refers to all the extra costs of organic produce, i.e. additional
   growing, transportation, packaging and distribution costs.
6 (i) **This** in 'This has meant that' refers to the fact that until now organic
       farming has been carried out by enthusiasts rather than by
       commercially-minded business people.
   (ii) **This situation** refers to (a) the increased costs incurred by organic
       producers and (b) the amateur approach to organic farming.
   (iii) **These problems** refers to the increased costs and amateur
       approach of organic farmers.
   (iv) **They** means 'the multiples'.
   (v) **One** means 'one of the two major factors that leads to the very
       high price of organic produce'.
   (vi) **It** in 'than it is here' means 'the organic market'.

Chapter 8
Reading skills

A fair number of candidates believed that they were explaining why the sources differed when they were only describing the differences.

(From the Report on the 1989 History GCSE examinations, Northern Examining Association)

When candidates answer examination questions they must have a crystal clear idea of what a **description** is, what an **explanation** is, of **examples**, of **methods** and so on. These are some of the 'building blocks' or components of which every piece of writing is made up. To read properly you must distinguish each of these features and understand them fully.

This chapter therefore, gives practice in (a) identifying the most important types of text component and (b) recognizing words that signal their presence.

● **GENERAL POINTS AND PARTICULAR POINTS**

Particular points often follow a general one. For example:

This painting is about parting. *– General point*

The central figure looking up is leaving this world, and the figure holding her is trying to stop her from going. The face looking down from above is someone who's already departed – now a spirit or an angel. It's a very personal image really.

Particular points

(Phyllis Mahon in *Spare Rib*, November 1990)

The particular point is often an **example** of the general one. The distinction between general and particular is important because it is nearly always the **general** points that should be written down in a summary or included in a set of notes.

PRACTICE

Identify the general and particular points in these texts:

Extract A

The meat and poultry industry also rejects allegations about the maltreatment of animals bred for slaughter.

'Most sheep and beef cattle are reared in grassy fields', says Geoff Harrington, Director of Research for the Meat and Livestock Commission. 'If they're brought in during winter they're kept in airy places, with plenty of straw. Twenty per cent of sows are now reared outside as well.'

(From 'Vegetarianism', *Prime Time*, November 10, 1990)

Extract B

The personal computer is becoming more musical as a result of two innovations developed in the last decade. The first, known as sequencing, allows someone to rearrange the bars of a musical composition precisely as one rearranges paragraphs of writing on the computer screen. The second is called sampling, a technique that takes a small bit of prerecorded sound – anything from a complete vocal track to a single drumbeat – and then manipulates it into a new sound. For example: in the last *Indiana Jones* film, when Harrison Ford found himself surrounded by thousands of rats, the chirping of the rats had nothing in common with rodents. The sound was actually a gaggle of upset geese, sampled and sped up to sound like tiny mammals.

(From 'Sound Bytes, Neon Dreams', M. Rogers, *Newsweek*, November 5, 1990)

● EXAMPLES

These are signalled in many different ways (**for example, for instance, such as, e.g.,** by the use of dashes), but sometimes there is no expression to indicate that an example is present. Think in terms of:

- the point which is going to be exemplified.
- words that signal an example.
- the example itself.

For example:

point to be exemplified ⎰ Different species have their own ways of ⎱ revealing their strengths – red deer stags,——first

signal———— for example , will roar at each other, and example
stag beetles will display their horns

second example (From *BBC Wildlife*, June 1990)

PRACTICE

Read this text and answer the questions that follow it.

The Sumerians, who lived in what is now Iraq, invented a system of writing about 3100 B.C. They scratched their words on pieces of clay. Most of their early clay tablets record practical data such as lists of agricultural produce. Later on, people who could read and write sent each other personal messages. One, for example, is signed 'your loving wife who has had a child'. Many other clay tablets recorded important matters of state like royal decrees and laws.

(Based on *The Age of God-Kings*, Time-Life Books)

1 (a) *What is mentioned as an example of practical data recorded by the Sumerians?*

(b) What expression introduces this example?

2 The second example in the text includes the words 'your loving wife . . .'. What is this an example of?

3 The last sentence includes examples.
(a) What are the examples?
(b) What word introduces them?
(c) What are they examples of?

Read the following and answer the questions that follow it.

Many people – environmentalists, bankers, lawyers and diplomats – are searching for the magic formula which could allow some kind of international deal to save the forests.

Two major international initiatives are the International Tropical Timber Organization (ITTO) – a club of nations that consume or produce tropical timber – and the Tropical Forestry Action Plan (TFAP), a scheme backed by the World Bank and UN agencies that would channel aid money towards national forestry plans. The ITTO, heavily lobbied by green groups such as the World Wide Fund for Nature and Friends of the Earth, is backing sustainable forestry schemes.

(From 'Rainforest Supplement', *BBC Wildlife*, June 1990)

1 Give examples of types of people who are looking for a worldwide scheme to save forests.

2 Are these examples signalled in any way?

3 Numbers often introduce examples.
(a) What examples are introduced by a number in this text?
(b) Of what are they examples?

4 The last sentence includes examples.
(a) What words signal these examples?
(b) Quote the examples.
(c) Of what are they examples?

Other expressions that signal the presence of an example include: 'a **typical** .... is ....'; 'We can **illustrate** this by ....'; 'an **illustration** of ....'; '............. **shows/demonstrates** ....'; '**include** ....'; 'to make this **clearer**, we can **look** at ....'.

● SAYING 'HOW'

Many words signal a method, telling us **how** something is done. The word **method** is one of them; **by** is another, often followed by a verb ending in **-ing**. Where a text gives a method or way, it must be a way of **doing something**.

PRACTICE

*Read this text and answer the questions that follow it. It is about birds called **turnstones**, a Dr Philip Whitfield was studying them.*

A total of six different feeding methods were observed being used. In some cases, choice was fairly obviously influenced by habitat. **Stone-turning**, for example, was used mainly on pebbly parts of the shore or when searching in rock pools. Birds looking for prey among piles of seaweed tended to feed by **routing** – flicking or bulldozing the seaweed aside to uncover tiny amphipod shellfish or small molluscs. At the water's edge **probing** was the technique used when searching among seaweed.

(From *BBC Wildlife*, June 1990)

1 How many feeding methods have been mentioned so far?

2 List these methods. In what three letters does each end?

*3 What two words are used to signal the presence of a **way** of doing something?*

● CAUSE AND EFFECT

Read this text:

> Our native otter population has declined catastrophically since about 1950 because of a variety of causes: pollution of its rivers and lakes, disturbance, clearance of riverside vegetation and hunting.
> (From *Environment Now*, March 1990)

This text includes these elements:

- CAUSES – pollution, disturbance, clearance.
- an EFFECT – decline of the otter population.
- a SIGNAL of this RELATIONSHIP – because of a variety of causes.

Similar to a **cause** is a **reason** for something, as in this extract:

> When you have made your pond, plants can be put into it after allowing a few days for the water to clear. A water lily is worth having, for besides the beauty of the flowers, its large leaves will shade the water and reduce the build-up of algae.
> (From *Environment Now*, March 1990)

In this text **for** tells us **why** the water lily is worth having. How many **reasons** are given?

The words **explain** and **explanation** are often used in exam questions and mean that in answers reasons must be given.

PRACTICE

These texts show some of the many ways of expressing a cause/effect relationship. In each case look for:

–the cause
–the effect
–word(s) that signal this relationship

Answer the questions that follow each extract.

Extract A

> Anyone who has visited the remoter parts of Scotland, and particularly the islands, will know that old abandoned cars and farm vehicles are all too common. It is difficult for people in these areas to dispose of old vehicles, so they just get left to rot. They are unsightly and potentially dangerous.
> (From *Environment Now*, March 1990)

1 What is the cause?
2 What is the effect?
3 What word signals the relationship?
4 Does this word come before the cause or the effect?

Extract B

> In the fifties, when most of the national parks were created, no one envisaged the levels of car ownership which we have today. People who own a car need something to do with it. What could be more natural than visiting a national park?
>   One result of this situation was a six-mile traffic jam outside the town of Windermere on the May Bank Holiday last year.
> (From *Environment Now*, March 1990)

1 What is the cause?
2 What is the effect?
3 What word signals the relationship?

Some of the many other ways of indicating a cause include: 'factor'; 'can be attributed to . . .'; 'due to . . .'. And these are further ways of indicating an effect: 'lead(s) to . . .'; 'bring(s) about . . .'; 'account(s) for . . .'.

● DEFINITION

In your studies you will meet a great many new ideas, words and phrases and each one will have a definition. In exams you may be asked to provide your own definitions. Here are examples from a biology paper:

1 What does the term **fertilization** mean?
2 What does the term **diffusion** mean?

You might answer **2** as follows:

Diffusion is a random movement of molecules from a region where they are concentrated to a region where they are less concentrated.

Definitions are exceedingly important because they give you the meaning of ideas that are vital to a topic you are studying. So look out for them as you read. To help you recognize them, these are some of the ways in which definitions are expressed:

1 (a) 'X (word to be defined) **is** a y **which** . . .'
E.g. An element **is** a pure substance **which** cannot be split up by chemical reaction.
(b) 'This (referring to something mentioned in the previous sentence) is a y which . . .'
2 (a) 'A y **which** . . . is known as X'
' . . . is called X'
E.g. A catalyst **which** slows down a reaction **is called** a negative catalyst or inhibitor.
(b) Similar to (a), often at the end of a short paragraph, and starting with **this, they, it**, etc.
E.g. One of the most eye-catching ways of illustrating statistics is to make your graph in the form of a picture. **This** kind of graph **is called** a pictograph or pictogram.
3 'X, **that is**, . . .'
E.g.

More than half of all the antibiotics administered to farm animals are given to pigs. But many of these animals are not even suffering from a disease; the antibiotics are administered as a prophylactic dose, **that is**, a treatment to prevent infection rather than to treat an existing illness.
(From *Green Magazine*, June 1990)

Where to find definitions

Early in the presentation of a new topic, often in the first sentence of a paragraph or at the end of a paragraph.

A definition is frequently followed by an **example**, which is given in order to make the meaning of the definition even clearer.

PRACTICE

1 Find two definitions in the passage below and write them out.

*2 Say which of the types of definition listed above (**1, 2** and **3**) each is like in the way it is expressed.*

One of the most popular ready meals is chicken tikka. This is an Indian dish which consists of small pieces of chicken soaked in spices and baked in a tandoor oven. It has helped make Indian food popular. The tandoor is an egg-shaped clay oven which is rather like an enormous Ali Baba pot. It is about five feet high, narrowing to a hole at the top.
(Based on *BBC Good Food*, May 1990)

1 Identify and write out each definition in the text that follows.

2 Say which of the types of definition listed above (1, 2 and 3) each resembles in the way it is expressed.

3 List the examples that occur in the text.

The Effect of Electricity on Chemicals

Conductors and insulators

A substance which allows electricity to pass through it is called a **conductor**. Of the solid elements at room temperature, only metals and graphite (a form of carbon) are good conductors. They conduct electricity because electrons pass freely through the solid.

Substances which do not allow electricity to pass through are called **insulators**. Some substances e.g. germanium, conduct electricity slightly and are called **semiconductors**. They are important for making transistors.

Electrolytes

Certain substances do not conduct electricity when solid but do when molten or dissolved in water. They are called **electrolytes**. However, the passage of electricity through the melt or solution is accompanied by a chemical decomposition. The splitting up of an electrolyte, when molten or in aqueous solution, is called **electrolysis**.

Electrolytes include: acids, metal oxides, metal hydroxides and salts.

Electrolytes are composed of **ions** but in the solid state the ions are rigidly held in regular positions and are unable to move to an electrode. Sodium chloride is composed of a regular lattice of sodium Na^+ and chloride$^-$ CL ions.

Melting the electrolyte breaks down the forces between the ions. The ions are, therefore, free to move in a molten electrolyte. In molten sodium chloride the sodium and chloride ions are able to move freely.

Dissolving an electrolyte in water (or other polar solvent) also causes the breakdown of the Lattice and again the ions are free to move.

(From *Revise GCSE Chemistry*, B. McDuell, Charles Letts & Co Ltd)

● DESCRIPTION

After a definition, and sometimes an example or two, a text often continues with a description. This gives further information about a thing, e.g. its properties or characteristics. It may state which parts a thing has, what it consists of, what it can do, its function and so on.

Answer the questions that follow. They relate to the text above: 'The Effect of Electricity on Chemicals'

1 What descriptive information is given about metals and graphite at room temperature?

2 Quote the words that state what electrolytes consist of.

3 What information is given about electrolytes in their solid state?

4 The parts of a particular substance are given. What substance is this?

Find descriptions in two of your textbooks, e.g. a description of a person in a history textbook or novel, a description in a science text.

Description of a process

Another important type of description is description of a process. These examination questions ask you to describe a process:

1 Describe the process of nitrogen fixation which goes on in the swellings (nodules) on the roots of some types of green plant.

2 Describe the pathway of the nerve impulses in a spinal reflex.

3 Outline briefly how sulphur is produced commercially.

Each of these processes consists of a series of steps or stages. When you describe them, you state the stages in the order in which they happen. Look out for processes when you read and try to think of each as consisting of a particular number of steps. This will help you to remember them. Here are some processes from everyday life:

- making a pot of tea.
- changing a car wheel.
- making a video recording.
- cooking a meal.
- growing a crop of vegetables.

For example, these are the steps involved in making a cup of tea:

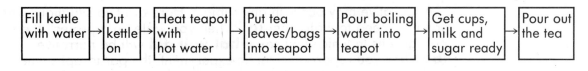

| Fill kettle with water | → | Put kettle on | → | Heat teapot with hot water | → | Put tea leaves/bags into teapot | → | Pour boiling water into teapot | → | Get cups, milk and sugar ready | → | Pour out the tea |

PRACTICE

1 Add three more everyday processes to the above list.

2 Choose one of your processes and divide it into stages. Present them as a flow chart.

3 Read the biology text below and name the process which it describes.

4 How many steps does this process consist of?

*5 The names of many processes end in –**tion** or –**sion**, e.g.* **vegetative reproduction***. Name a few more with these endings.*

If you put your hand on a hot plate, you pull it away quickly. This is an example of a **reflex action**. A reflex action is an immediate response of the body to a stimulus. Many other reflexes are shown by humans and other animals. For example, if you tap your knee in a certain place, your leg gives a little kick. This is called the **knee jerk**, and it is often used by doctors to find out if the patient's spinal cord is working properly. Another well-known reflex is the scratching movement of the hind leg of a dog when you tickle its tummy.

Let's consider what happens when you pull your hand away from a hot object. First of all, sensory endings in your fingers are stimulated by the heat. This causes impulses to pass up the nerve in your arm to the spinal cord and brain: the actual feeling of pain occurs when the impulses reach the brain. Further impulses then pass back down the arm to the muscles, causing them to contract. The contraction of the muscles has the effect of pulling your arm away from the unpleasant stimulus. The whole response only takes a fraction of a second and this shows how quickly the impulses travel through the nervous system.

The reflex arc

Scientists have worked out the route by which impulses travel through the nervous system in bringing about a reflex action. This comprises what we call a **reflex arc**.

The structure of the reflex arc involved in pulling your hand away from a hot object is shown in Figure 4. It is made up of five distinct parts:

1 A **receptor** which receives the stimulus. In this reflex the receptors are the sensory endings in the skin.

2 A **sensory nerve fibre** which carries impulses from the sensory endings to the spinal cord.

65

3 An **intermediate nerve fibre** which carries the impulses from the upper to the lower side of the spinal cord.

4 A **motor nerve fibre** which carries the impulses from the spinal cord to the muscle.

5 An **effector** which responds when impulses reach it. In this reflex the effector is the muscle in the arm.

(From *Biology for Life*, M.B.V. Roberts, Nelson)

● NARRATIVE

A narrative is like a description of a process in several respects: both give an account of a set of events in the order in which they happen. But whereas a process describes the way things **regularly** happen, a narrative relates what happened **on only one occasion**.

Narrative, in this chapter, means only those parts of a history or story or other text that deal with sets of events. It does not include description of people, places or situations.

A narrative may occur in any subject. Here are two situations where you may need to write one: **(a)** When you write up a project, the paragraphs in which you say **what you did** will be narratives. **(b)** When you report a scientific experiment, the paragraphs where you say what you did, what happened and what you observed are narratives.

PRACTICE

1 Look for stretches of narrative in a novel you are familiar with.

2 Find a passage in which a set of events is narrated in one of your textbooks.

Warning: in examinations there is a tendency for candidates to write narratives when some other kind of writing, e.g. an explanation, is required. Always be aware of such differences.

● ADDITION

When you read, it is of value to you to be able to take conscious note of when the writer is **adding** a new point to a previous point or set of points. For example, a writer may state **one** method of obtaining sulphur and then add a **second** method. You, the reader, need to appreciate that **two** methods are being given. It will help you to notice where the second begins if you are used to looking out for words that **signal** it.

PRACTICE

*In the texts that follow, which words signal that the writer is presenting **another** point additional to a previous one just mentioned?*

Extract A

Hydrogen can be prepared by the action of dilute sulphuric acid on zinc.
It is also produced when certain metals react with water and when zinc and aluminium react with alkalis.
Most hydrogen used in industry is produced from natural gas.

(From *Revise GCSE Chemistry*, B. McDuell, Charles Letts & Co Ltd)

Extract B

You will no doubt be familiar with the services offered by your own school library. Similar services are offered at the local library and the central library in your nearest large town. Apart from **lending** books, however, libraries have several other purposes. You can use them as reference sources . . .

(From *Geography Coursework Companion*, N. Law, Charles Letts & Co Ltd)

Now look through your own textbooks and find expressions that introduce an additional point. You may find words like these: **another, further, in addition, added to this is the fact that, moreover, too**.

When you present a set of similar points in a paragraph or essay, you will make yourself clearer to your reader—to the examiner—if you introduce each additional one with a suitable expression. **Also** is probably the commonest.

● COMPARE AND CONTRAST

'Compare and contrast' questions are a favourite with teachers and examiners. Try and notice when a text is contrasting one point with another and when it is making a comparison. Here are some expressions that signal a contrast: **but, however, whereas, although, nevertheless, yet, on the other hand**.

Here are some forms of language that signal a comparison:

1 Any of the expressions that signal a contrast.

2 Any words that imply comparison, e.g. **better, bigger, cheaper, more** efficient, **less** complicated, (not) **as . . . as . . .**

3 Words such as these: **similar, compared with, the same as, like, unlike, different, differ, resemble, identical**.

PRACTICE

Read the following passage and answer the questions that follow:

Avocado trees are extremely thirsty, needing twice as much water as do orange trees, yet only producing one tenth of the fruit. What is more, they are very fussy about what they will drink, requiring pure water with a minimum dosage of chlorine and sodium.

There are three basic root stocks: one from Mexico, one from Guatemala and one from the West Indies. The West Indian one is less fussy about what it drinks, but produces unappealing avocados in relatively small quantities. So Mexican or Guatemalan trees are grafted onto West Indian root stock. But the West Indian root stock is even more sensitive to cold than the other two, so you stand a better chance of losing it in a cold snap . . .

Avocados have to be picked by hand, as machinery damages them and since the fruits do not all reach the same size at the same time the pickers have to go back again and again. Moreover, since the avocados are an identical green to the leaves of the trees, they are difficult to see and pick: an orange stands out much more clearly.

And if you want to know who eats them, according to official figures we do fairly well at an average of 350 g (about one and a half avocados) per person per year, as against the Germans 170 g. The French on the other hand get through 1.5 kilos (six avocados), and the Israelis an average of four kilos (16 avocados) per year, whereas in Mexico, where they originally came from, the unofficial, although probably quite accurate, estimate of consumption is 35 kilos or 140 avocados per person per year.

(From *Environment Now*, March 1990)

1 (a) In the first sentence, what two things are compared?
  (b) They are compared in respect of two features. What are these two features?
  (c) What expression gives you a clue that a comparison is being made?

2 (a) In the second paragraph, what words alert you to the presence of comparisons?
  (b) What things are compared?
  (c) What features are the comparisons concerned with?

3 In the last paragraph, what words signal comparisons and contrasts?

4 Leaving aside contrasts and comparisons, what sort of point is signalled by:
    (i) 'What is more' (first paragraph)?
    (ii) 'Moreover' (third paragraph)?
    What do the points that follow 'what is more' and 'moreover' have in common with the points that come before these expressions?

5 In one of your textbooks find a passage that includes one or more comparisons. Analyse them as the comparisons above have been analysed.

● TEXT THAT CLASSES THINGS

This section may be more applicable to you if you are a GCSE student.

A text may tell you that two or more things (e.g. oranges and apples) belong to a certain class of things (fruit, in this case). This is classification. Another example is shown by this quotation: 'Political systems vary. Democracies are based upon authority, and dictatorships are based upon power.' In other words, democracies and dictatorships are two members of the class (or category) of things called political systems.

After reading the extract below, try answering the two questions. Most of the text is about an important concept and the 'members' of it.
    1 What is the concept?
    2 What are the members of it?

Power and authority

Power is when a person or a group forces other people to do what they want, for example, a kidnapper.

Authority is when a person or group is obeyed because others believe that it is right and correct that they should be obeyed, for example, teacher and pupils.

There are three different types of authority:

1 **Charismatic** people are obeyed because they have a particular personality that people feel is awe-inspiring, for example, Jesus Christ.

2 **Traditional** people are obeyed because they have always been obeyed, for example, parents.

3 **Legal-rational** people are obeyed because they hold a particular position in an organization, for example, a manager of an office.

In reality the three types of authority are usually mixed together. In our daily lives we are constantly meeting situations of power and authority and they influence the way we act. In the family, in school, at work – all are examples of where power and authority are in action. Usually we are happy to obey when an act is seen as based upon authority, but not when it is based upon power.

The words **kinds** and **sorts** are also used to introduce classes of people, things or ideas. The presence of a number in the text is sometimes an indication, too.

● CONCLUSION

When you have a set of facts and you apply your mind to them, you often reach a conclusion. For example:

Fact 1 There was a cricket match.
Fact 2 It began to rain.

Fact 3 Cricketers don't play in the rain.

Conclusion: Therefore they stopped playing.

A conclusion often comes towards the end of a paragraph or group of paragraphs and is introduced by expressions like **so, therefore, then, this means that, thus, hence** and the word **result**.

PRACTICE

1 What conclusion is there in the second paragraph of the text about avocados (page 67)? What word introduces it?

2 Can you find a conclusion in the text on 'The Effect of Electricity on Chemicals' (p. 64)? What word introduces it?

● SUMMING UP

As you have seen, you use many skills when you read. The way to consolidate all these in your own mind is through **practice**. Read through a few past examination papers. Can you find questions asking for examples, methods/ways, causes and consequences, etc? You may see expressions like these:

- give a different **reason** in each case **why** . . .
- **describe** and **account for** the trends in . . .
- give an **example** of ill health . . .
- **compare** and **contrast** social discrimination in . . .
- explain **how** . . .
- what **effects** may . . . have on . . . ?

In your own writing use some of the signals for contrasts, comparisons, examples, methods and so on that you have been introduced to in this chapter. You are in a position to add variety to your writing and make it more interesting. Not only that, if you do signal causes, examples, and so on as such, you make your writing much clearer. The teachers, moderators and examiners who read your work and find it easier to understand will give you better marks.

Most candidates were able to distinguish between arteries and veins. Some expressed their answers either in tabular form or by coupling their differences with the word 'whereas'; this made it absolutely clear they were emphasizing the differences, in contrast to candidates who first described an artery with a diagram and then a vein with another diagram, leaving the examiner to pick out the differences.

(From the Report on the 1988 Biological Sciences A level examinations, Cambridge University Local Examinations Syndicate)

ANSWERS

Practice on page 60

Extract A: first sentence is general; the others are particular.
Extract B: first sentence is general; second particular; third particular; fourth and fifth are a particular example of the third sentence.

Practice on page 60

1 (a) Lists of agricultural produce.
  (b) 'such as'.
2 A personal message.
3 (a) 'royal decrees and laws'.
  (b) 'like'.
  (c) 'important matters of state'.

Advanced practice on page 61

1 Environmentalists, bankers, lawyers, diplomats.

2 By dashes.
3 (a) ITTO and TFAP.
  (b) Major international initiatives to save the forests.
4 (a) 'such as'.
  (b) World Wide Fund for Nature, Friends of the Earth.
  (c) Green groups that lobby the ITTO.

Practice on page 61
1 Three. 2 'Stone-turning', 'routing', 'probing'. 3 'methods', 'technique'.

Practice on page 62

Extract A

1 The difficulty of getting rid of old vehicles.
2 Old vehicles are left to rot.
3 'so'.
4 Before the effect.

Extract B

1 The fact that many car owners decided to visit national parks.
2 A six-mile traffic jam outside Windermere.
3 'result'.

Practice on page 63

1 (i) 'This is an Indian dish which consists of small pieces of chicken
     soaked in spices and baked in a tandoor oven.'
   (ii) 'The tandoor is an egg-shaped clay oven which is rather like an
     enormous Ali Baba pot.'
2 1 (i) is like definition **1**(b) in the list.
  1 (ii) is like definition **1**(a) in the list.

Advanced practice on page 64

1 and 2 : Sentence beginning:
        'A substance which . . .' – type **2**(a);
        'Substances which do not . . .' – type **2**(a);
        'Some substances . . .' – type **2**(a);
        'They are called . . .' – type **2**(b);
        'The splitting up . . .' – type **2**(a).
3 Examples: 1 'metals and graphite' (examples of solid elements at room
                temperature which are good conductors).
            2 'germanium' (of a semiconductor).
            3 'acids', etc (of electrolytes).

Practice on page 64

1 They are good conductors
2 'Electrolytes are composed of ions'.
3 'The ions are rigidly held in regular positions and are unable to move
  to an electrode.'
4 Sodium chloride.

Practice on page 65

3 **reflex action**. 4 Five steps. 5 Fertilization, an election.

Practice on page 66

Extract A
'also', 'and'.

Extract B
'apart from', 'other'.

Practice on page 67

1 (a) Avocado trees and orange trees.
  (b) The amount of water they need, the amount of fruit they yield.
  (c) 'Twice as much . . . as . . .'.
2 (a) '**less** fussy', '**more** sensitive . . . **than** . . .'.
  (b) Avocado root stocks.
  (c) The purity of water required, amount of fruit, reaction to cold.
3 'as against', 'on the other hand', 'whereas'.
4 Additional points. The points in question are difficult aspects of avocados.

Practice on page 68

1 Types of authority. 2 Charismatic people, traditional people, legal-rational people.

Practice on page 69

1 In a cold snap you are more likely to lose avocados grown on West Indian root stock; 'so'.
2 The ions are free to move in a molten electrolyte; 'therefore'.

Chapter 9
Bias and balance

THE PURPOSE OF THIS CHAPTER

Many authorities on education stress the need when studying texts to: detect bias; notice lack of evidence; notice gaps and inconsistencies; and assess how useful or reliable a source is.

This chapter, therefore, aims to:

● Stress the importance of hearing **both** sides of an issue
● State the need to reach a balanced judgement
● Show ways of discovering bias: by considering:

    (a) the **origin** of what you see or read
    (b) its **language**
    (c) the **evidence** or **reasons** put forward to support statements
    (d) the **selection** of information

● HEAR BOTH SIDES

Imagine that there has been a car accident and that you are the first on the scene. However, you didn't see it actually happen. One of the drivers gives his account of it and he puts the blame entirely on the other driver. Do you believe him without any question? No. You **expect** him to give an account which puts himself in the clear, so you decide to suspend judgement: you will not make up your mind about whose fault the accident was until you have heard at least what the other driver has to say.

Another example. Before a court decides on the guilt or innocence of an accused person, it hears **both** what the prosecuting counsel has to say **and** what the defending counsel has to say. **Evidence** of witnesses on both sides is heard and they are examined. Only then does the court make up its mind and deliver its verdict.

When you read books, articles and other sources, for example, in history, English, economics, on politics, the environment, crime and punishment, right and wrong, sex and business, then you do need to ask yourself 'Is the writer correct and is this account balanced?' A biased writer or cartoonist does not take another viewpoint fully into account. He puts over mainly his own view, possibly in strong terms. It is necessary to study carefully **all** the facts and see that they have been interpreted fairly.

● REACH A BALANCED JUDGEMENT

How should you react when confronted with a one-sided account? Having a mind of your own, you should at least **consider** opposing arguments or else be thought unreasonable. When you read material on controversial topics, you should look out for bias or you risk being biased yourself if you swallow everything uncritically.

If you do suspect that a text, cartoon, map, etc is biased, you should:

● suspend judgement.
● find a source that gives the other point of view.

- reach a reasoned, balanced conclusion of your own. It is more important that you should provide good evidence and well-reasoned arguments than that you should adopt one viewpoint rather than another.

● HOW TO SPOT BIAS

1 Look at the **origin** of the material.

For example, if you pick up *The Daily Telegraph* newspaper and read a political topic, you can expect that it will be biased towards a conservative viewpoint.

PRACTICE

What viewpoint would you expect to find:

1 In a book about the Falklands War written by an Argentinian army officer?

2 In an article about industrial pollution or 'greenhouse gases' in a Greenpeace publication? Would you, for example, expect such an article to give full weight to commercial considerations, to play them down or ignore them altogether?

3 In an article about Scottish independence from Westminster rule written by a member of the Scottish Nationalist Party?

2 Look at the **language** of the material.

Here is a situation: toxic waste is often shipped from the country where it is produced to another country which has facilities for its disposal. There is an article in *Green* magazine about this trade in toxic waste entitled 'Leper Ships'. Do these words give you a clue about the attitude of the writer? An introductory sentence says 'Industrial nations have been exporting waste, at the rate of one cargo every five minutes, but a global backlash has toxic traders on the run.' What attitude do 'global backlash' and 'has toxic traders on the run' suggest to you? Are there two sides to this question?

'Guerrillas' is a fairly neutral word for armed men who fight not as a regular army, but by living off the land making surprise attacks. The same people could be referred to by one writer as 'freedom fighters' and by another as 'terrorists'. Do such expressions tell you more about the guerrillas or about the views of the writer?

PRACTICE

Here is a source from a history exam. Which words in it warn you that there may be bias in it?

A table of figures published in a Chinese newspaper in 1970. UN General Assembly votes on the restoration of China's legal rights in the UN 1950–1970.

	1950	1955	1960	1965	1970
Votes supporting China	10	12	34	47	51
Votes siding with US Imperialists	37	41	41	46	48
Abstentions	8	6	22	20	25

Notes:

1 Votes siding with US Imperialists do not include that of the Chiang-Kai-Shek Bandit Gang which illegally occupies China's seat.
2 In 1964, no discussion on any draft resolution was held because of US imperial obstruction.

(From GCSE History Paper 2, Syllabus B, June 1989, Northern Examining Association)

3 Look at the **evidence** or **reasons** that are put forward to support the writer's view. Make sure that there **are** reasons and that they are good enough.

PRACTICE

Consider together extracts A and B and answer these questions.

1 Extract A states that the number of cases of salmonella is comparatively small. (a) What evidence, if any, does it give to support this general statement? (b) Do you accept this general statement? (c) Bearing in mind that a government might wish to play down a health scare, what effect do the following words have on you 'but this underestimates the numbers'?

2 (a) What evidence does extract B offer to support its statement that fluoride is dangerous? (b) Given that some water authorities add fluoride to water supplies, what judgement do you make about its dangers?

*3 In extract B: (a) Are the reasons offered for giving up the various listed foods adequate? (b) What is meant by calling canned foods (e.g. baked beans) **dead**? Do baked beans have **no value**? (c) Are **all** additives poisons?*

4 In general, if a text makes a general statement and does not support it with evidence, does this mean that the statement is false?

Extract A

Eggs. The facts

Eggs are a valuable and nutritious part of a balanced diet. We in Britain eat, on average, 30 million eggs a day – 200 million a week. The number of reported cases of food poisoning from salmonella linked to eggs is very small by comparison with the huge numbers of eggs that are consumed.

So far this year there have been 49 reported outbreaks of salmonella traced back to eggs. These outbreaks affected 1000 people, but this underestimates the numbers.

The Government and industry are tackling the problem and, among other things, have issued codes of practice for poultry breeders and egg producers.

(Government advertisement, 18th December, 1988)

Extract B

Not only should you be aware of how your food was grown, but also of what goes into your drinking water. Fluoride, for instance, is a dangerous chemical adding yet more to the work load your body has to get through. We believe fluoride to be a highly poisonous chemical and if it has been added to your water, we recommend that you try bottled spring water for use in cooking and for drinking.

Give up	Reason why	Change to
All canned, smoked, bottled, preserved, manufactured and synthetic products and flavourings.	Dead food has no value and the additives are positively harmful. They are poisons.	Fresh, raw, homemade whole foods.

4 If reasons, evidence and facts are given, look at the **selection** of reasons, evidence and facts. If they are all on one side only, you may suspect that the writer is biased and that he or she may have left out important information.

Here are two examples from daily life where a writer may select only favourable facts:

(a) Estate agents sending out particulars of houses which they have for sale. They might describe a garden as 'delightful' or 'well-stocked', but not say that there is a busy dual carriageway a few yards from it or a smelly pig farm next door. They might mention old beams, but not the rot or beetles in the woodwork. If a lot of expensive work needs to be done, then a house has 'a lot of potential'. And so on.

(b) Tour operators describing hotels at foreign resorts. They are not likely to mention, for example, that a hotel is surrounded by noisy building sites. And if the sea water is polluted, they may well keep quiet about it.

PRACTICE

In the mid-1930s Italy invaded and controlled Abyssinia (now Ethiopia). The League of Nations took ineffective action to end their occupation. The following text is from an Italian school textbook of 1937. In what way does it show bias?

We have shown the world that we are the strong ones, the just ones, the best ones. The fifty two nations, which imposed sanctions against Italy, refused us bread, iron, gold, coal and cloth. We have found it all anyway. They wanted to humiliate us, but our victory and sacrifice have raised us above them.

(From GCSE History Paper 2, Syllabus B, June 1989, Northern Examining Association)

If you do detect bias in a text, this does not necessarily mean that it is useless as, for example, an historical source. If an article in a colour supplement shows bloody pictures of whales being cut up, this may indicate bias, but it also tells you that a great many people object to the killing of whales, which it may be important to know.

PRACTICE

Consider extracts A, B and C together.

1 Does any language in extract A suggest that it is biased?

2 Does the source of the text alert you to the possibility of bias?

3 Is there any type of information missing from extract A which you think ought to be included to make it balanced?

4 Do you have any other comments on the bias or balance of this text?

5 Contrast what extracts B and C say about the greenhouse effect of 134A.

6 Contrast what the two texts say about ICI's intentions concerning the phasing out of CFCs.

7 What attitude is it wise to adopt in the light of your answers to questions 5 and 6?

8 (a) What is the implication in extract C of its point that in order to phase out CFCs completely, alternative products must be found?

(b) What does this contrast with in the last paragraph of extract B?

9 What is the force, in extract C, of 'For we all still rely on CFCs for many of life's essentials'?

10 Why does extract B, but not extract C, mention the quantities of chemicals produced?

11 Why does extract C but not extract B mention the efforts of researchers?

Extract A

ICI – Ozone Destroyers

The destruction of the Ozone layer has not been stopped. Every year more than a million tonnes of ozone destroyers are produced, despite the Montreal Protocol, an international agreement to protect the ozone layer. The Montreal Protocol will allow 50% more ozone destroyers than already exist to be manufactured before they are finally banned.

In the UK, ICI are the biggest producers of ozone destroyers: they produce 80% of the CFCs and are major producers of methyl chloroform and carbon tetrachloride, two other powerful ozone destroyers. Greenpeace wants the production and use of all these chemicals stopped now. To show that you share our concern, put this sticker in a prominent place in your home or car. Show ICI (and all producers of ozone destroyers) that there is no place in the "green decade" ahead for a company which produces chemicals known to cause such great environmental damage.

(From a *Greenpeace* article, April 1990)

Extract B

ICI still produces at least 200 000 tonnes of ozone destroyers every year. According to the most recent comparative data, ICI is the largest producer of CFCs in Western Europe, the largest Western European producer of methyl chloroform, and produces thousands of tonnes of carbon tetrachlorides.

The Department of the Environment has stated that since 1984 there has been unequivocal evidence that serious stratospheric ozone depletion is being caused by the emission of CFCs and halons.

CFCs are still used as solvents, refrigerants, foam blowing agents and in some aerosols. There are several available alternatives to these ozone destroyers. ICI is producing one particular alternative: HFC – 134A. It does no damage to the ozone layer, but is a greenhouse gas 2500 times more powerful than carbon dioxide. If similar substitutes take over the old CFC market and their production rises, these substitutes would be responsible for about a tenth of global warming in the next century.

In June, renegotiation of the Montreal Protocol, which regulates ozone destroyers, takes place in London. The UK and other governments are likely to delay the phase out of these chemicals, even though safer substitutes are available now. If industry has its way, CFCs, halons, and carbon tetrachloride, the principal ozone destroyers, will remain in use for another 10 years.

(From a *Greenpeace* article, April 1990)

Extract C

Today representatives from more than one hundred countries are meeting in London to discuss the protection of the ozone layer.

ICI supports firm worldwide action. We want to phase out CFCs completely and as quickly as possible. To achieve this we must find alternative products. For we all still rely on CFCs for many of life's essentials, such as the refrigeration of food and of blood for transfusions.

That is why ICI has devoted the skills of many of our best scientists and technologists to the search for alternatives to CFCs. And we're getting results. ICI is now a world leader in this field.

Our 'KLEA' 134A, for example, will replace CFCs in many types of refrigeration. It will be available next year and 'KLEA' will be totally ozone benign.

Replacing CFCs will also reduce the threat of global warming, CFCs contribute 14 per cent to the greenhouse effect. These new alternative products will contribute less than 1 per cent.

Anyone can talk about problems.

At ICI, we discover solutions.

(From an *ICI* advertisement in national newspapers, June 20, 1990)

ADVANCED PRACTICE

Read extracts A to E about whaling in order to answer the questions below.

Notes: 1 IWC stands for International Whaling Commission. This body regulates whaling and at times has imposed a moratorium, i.e. a temporary suspension, on 'commercial whaling'. Member countries can leave the IWC if they so wish and then hunt whales if they want to.

2 Minke are the smallest type of whale (about 8m long) and are comparatively numerous.

1 Does extract A attempt to be balanced or is it biased? Give a reason for your answer.

2 What words are used in extract B for hunting or killing whales? Are they emotive or neutral?

3 What words are used in extract C for hunting or killing whales? Are they emotive or neutral?

4 *The need to be consistent is expressed at the end both of extract B and extract D.*
   (a) Express this argument in your own words.
   (b) Is the making of this point a sign of bias or balance?

5 *Does the source of extract D lead you to expect it to be biased?*

6 *Extract C states 'Today, the whale is an endangered species.' Text D states 'In the minke whale's case, the question of endangerment has not yet been satisfactorily answered . . .'. Can you form any impression of bias or balance from such statements?*

7 *Extract E refers in its second paragraph to the motives behind Japanese whaling.*
   (a) Is evidence given?
   (b) What attitude do you adopt towards this attribution of motive?

8 *(a) What expressions are used in extract C to describe or refer to the killing of whales for 'scientific research'?*
   (b) Leaving aside the question of whether or not you agree with it, is language like this emotive or neutral?

9 *Extract B mentions the Japanese attitude to a return to commercial whaling. Is the inclusion of this point a sign of bias or balance?*

10 *In extract B, is the information about Steinar Bastesen and the conversation with him presented in a biased or balanced way?*

11 *Which texts do you feel attempt to be balanced and which do you feel are biased?*

Extract A

Some minke whales die instantly. Many take 10 minutes or so and others up to half an hour. This may be unsavoury to think about, but it must at least be put alongside the half hour or so that it takes each of millions of cod to drown in the air of a fisherman's deck. Few of the children who know how wicked whaling is have much scruple about their fish fingers.

Extract B

But Japan, Norway and Iceland? Surely they should not be whaling at all. This is where the small, family-owned business comes in. . . . Steinar Bastesen, chairman of the North Norwegian Small-whaler Association, described how he had gone bankrupt when the ban on minke whaling hit him.

These men seemed a world away from the scientists, politicians, lobbyists and journalists in whose hands part of their livelihoods lie. They don't pretend to be nobel savages, just people in inhospitable places living by the sea.

Weren't they necessarily cruel? Bastesen fiercely disputed the idea: 'I have a great respect for the whale. They are the smartest animal I've hunted. In the old days, killing them could take a long time. With a harpoon grenade it's very difficult to injure a whale: You either kill it or miss it.'

But aren't whales very special animals? 'They are a resource,' said Bastesen. 'They are like a horse or a cow. And I like those too.'

There was a sustained campaign by the Japanese last week to persuade the West that for the time being at least, and probably for ever, they do not want to go back to big ship commercial whaling.

They, too, have small, poor whaling communities in the northern extremity of their country, which, since the ban on the minke hunt, cannot even get social security because they only ever worked half a year. The delegation accuses the Anglo-Saxon world of arrogance in eating roast beef and frogs' legs, but denying them their own tradition.

(Extracts A and B from an article by R. North, *The Sunday Times*, July 8, 1990)

Extract C

YOU COULD STOP ICELAND SLAUGHTERING WHALES JUST BY TELLING THEM WHAT TO DO WITH THEIR FISH.

Since the Second World War, Iceland has killed some 18,000 whales. Today, the whale is an endangered species.

Yet, despite the International Whaling Commission's ban on commercial whaling, Iceland continues its bloody slaughter.

Last year alone they killed 78 whales under the thin guise of "scientific research."

As a protest against this masquerade, American and West German companies hit them where it hurts most.

Collectively they cancelled a massive 30 million pound order of fish, Iceland's major export.

On the other hand British companies, such as Birds Eye and Tesco, remain some of the world's largest importers of Icelandic fish.

However if they as companies and we as individuals joined the boycott the added pressure would almost certainly force Iceland to end its annual massacre.

All we have to do is pull our fingers out.

(Greenpeace advertisement in *The Sunday Times* colour supplement, April 9, 1989)

Extract D

Saving the Whale Family

The reputed intelligence of maritime mammals, their mysterious calls and beguiling smiles, have meant that dolphins, porpoises and whales are among the most anthropomorphized of creatures. Their slaughter is thus peculiarly horrible. Yet any appeal to the countries that still take part in hunting them will only succeed if it is rooted in science, not sentiment.

Commercial hunting of big whales has been banned since 1986. Japan and Iceland, with the backing of Norway, claim that the minke whale population has since increased enough for the ban to be lifted. The argument is political as much as scientific. Japan says whaling is an integral part of its culture, and whalemeat an important source of food. The West has no right to encroach on Japanese culture in this way. If the whale is not an endangered species the West should mind its own business.

All countries of the world have a legitimate interest – indeed a duty – to help stop a species from dying out. But they do not have a moral right to proscribe other countries' behaviour purely on the grounds of squeamishness. Moreover, such pressure would simply be counter-productive. Japan has chosen to be part of the IWC; it could easily pull out.

In the minke whale's case, the question of endangerment has not yet been satisfactorily answered. IWC scientists have been asked to come up with new ways of calculating how big the population must become before it is safe to start killing again without endangering the species.

Clearly unnecessary killing should not take place. But many maritime mammals are hunted for food. To win agreement from countries with a vested interest in killing these species, the other members of the commission must avoid emotional arguments. Western countries battery-farm their chickens, shoot gamebirds, force-feed geese, slaughter their sheep and cows, and rear their calves unnaturally to produce veal. If the Japanese choose to kill unendangered species, humanely, for food, other countries can hardly plead for restraint where they themselves show none.

(From the leading article in *The Times*, July 3, 1990)

Extract E

It's been calculated that whalemeat constitutes a fraction of one per cent of the protein intake of the Japanese people, therefore it's of the dietary relevance that caviar is to you or me.

So why is Japan still whaling commercially – albeit under the guise of 'scientific whaling'? Ottaway is adamant: 'They're doing it out of a perverse nationalism.' "We will not be dictated to," that's the fundamental message. It is not an issue to the Japanese people, there isn't much publicity about this inside Japan.

If anything is going on they dismiss it as "terrorism, Japan – bashing, racism" – that's how it's conveyed and there's no opportunity to put any other case.'

In reality, any arguments proposed in favour of a resumption of commercial whaling look appallingly weak. While Norway argues a strongly disputed case that minkes are depleting their fish stocks, it would be hard for them to claim that a fleet of whaling ships was laid-up and that unemployment was rife as a consequence. Similarly, Japan in 1990 has a relatively low investment in whaling ships, and only a small number of people employed in its industry.

(From an article in *Green* magazine, G. Cooper, July 1990)

ANSWERS

Practice on page 73

1 You would expect an anti-British, pro-Argentinian viewpoint. You would expect **policy** to be criticized, but not necessarily British forces themselves.

2 You might expect Greenpeace to show prejudice against industrial organizations and sometimes to play down or ignore costs.

3 You would expect it to favour Scottish independence and be against Westminster rule.

Practice on page 73

Words suggesting bias: 'siding with', 'Imperialists', 'Bandit Gang', 'illegally', 'US imperial obstruction'.

Practice on page 74

1 (a) To enable a comparison to be made the text states both the numbers of eggs eaten and the numbers of cases of salmonella. This is good evidence.
  (b) You must answer this for yourself.
  (c) One is inclined to believe a writer when he gives information that is not entirely favourable to him – it suggests honesty. But, of course, do not be tricked by a writer who understates the case against himself.

2 (a) No evidence against fluoride is given.
  (b) Conclude that the matter is controversial: suspend judgement while looking for more information about fluoride.

3 (a) The reasons are not adequate: they are sweeping and are themselves unsupported.
  (b) **Dead** might mean anything here. It is used more to arouse feelings against these foods than as a way of describing them. Baked beans do have value. Look at the label on a tin to see what they contain in the way of energy, protein, carbohydrate, fat, sodium and fibre.
  (c) It is certain that not all additives are poisons. Many are used after exhaustive scientific study of them. 'Poisons' is used to arouse our feelings against them.

4 No.

Practice on page 75

1 The text states that Italy is just. No evidence is given and considering that Italy is occupying another country, justification must be given.

2 The case against Italy is suppressed: the implication that sanctions were intended to humiliate Italy is not convincing.

Practice on page 75

1 The use of 'ozone destroyers' to refer to ICI.

2 The text is published by Greenpeace, well-known for its hostility to any possible threat to the environment.

3 The text states that there is 'no place in the "green decade" ahead' for a company which produces CFCs. It does not consider how we would manage without them (they are used in fridges).

5 Extract B says 134A is 2500 times more powerful than carbon dioxide. It would, therefore, contribute a lot to global warming. But extract C says 134A will contribute less than one per cent to the greenhouse effect (compared with 14 per cent contributed by the CFCs).

6 Text B says 'If industry has its way, CFCs . . . will remain in use for another 10 years', implying that the industry wishes to keep making them, whereas extract C says 'We want to phase out CFCs completely and as quickly as possible.'

7 The attitude of a careful reader should be:

   (i) to check facts if the subject is controversial (question 5 shows the two texts differ in matters of fact)
   (ii) to be very cautious when there is a statement of motives or intentions (as highlighted by question 6).

8 (a) This implies that alternatives to CFCs are not yet available.
   (b) This contrasts with 'safer substitutes are available now.' in the last paragraph of extract B.

9 This underlines the point that everyone in the community benefits from—in fact depends on—CFCs for some essentials.

10 Extract B mentions the quantities of chemicals to stress the amount of damage it claims is being done. Extract C does not mention amounts, partly, at least, because they would seem unfavourably large.

11 Extract C mentions the research effort because it makes readers think well of the company. Extract B avoids mentioning it because it does not want to give the company any credit for the efforts it is making.

Advanced practice on page 76

1 Extract A tries to be balanced. It compares the killing of whales to the killing of cod. From the point of view of their suffering there is little difference, so we should object to both or neither, in this regard.

2 'Whaling', 'hunted', 'killing': neutral expressions.

3 'Slaughtering', 'bloody slaughter', 'massacre': emotive expressions; 'killed': neutral.

4 (a) If we in the West obtain food from animals in ways that may seem cruel to others, we have no grounds for objecting when the Japanese do the same.
   (b) This statement is a sign of balance.

5 Extract D is from *The Times*. It is likely to attempt to be balanced.

6 The more general and unqualified a statement is, the more likely it is to be inaccurate and possibly biased. The first statement does not take the trouble to distinguish between different species of whale. The second statement is cautious and therefore unlikely to be biased.

7 (a) No evidence of Japanese motives is offered. The reader could be misled by the double quotation marks into thinking the words they enclose were spoken by Japanese people. But as this is not stated, it is almost certainly not the case.
   (b) It is wise to be cautious when motives are put forward, especially if they are not supported by evidence.

8 (a) 'the thin guise', 'this masquerade'.
   (b) Emotive.

9 It is a sign of balance.

10 In a balanced way.

11 Most opinions would agree that extracts A, B and D attempt to be balanced and that extracts C and E are biased.

Chapter 10
Making notes

THE PURPOSE OF THIS CHAPTER

The purpose of this chapter is, above all, to teach a good strategy for making notes, with the student's concentration focused on the central theme of a text. This is approached using the following sections:

- What are notes?
- Why make notes?
- How to go about making notes
- When to make notes
- What to note
- How to set out notes
- Indicate relations between points
- Use diagrams sometimes
- Use i.e., e.g., and so on
- Be accurate
- Organize your notes

● WHAT ARE NOTES?

Notes are a short clear statement of the essential points of a text or talk. For example:

TEXT: **What is poverty?**
There are two definitions of poverty: *absolute poverty* and *relative poverty*.

Absolute poverty
According to this definition, poverty is the condition of a person who has not got enough money to feed, clothe and house him/herself adequately. It was first used by researcher, Joseph Rowntree, in his studies of poverty between 1899 and 1950. Rowntree said that food, clothing and housing were essentials which everyone needs. He then found out just how much income was needed for a person to remain healthy, to clothe him/herself with the fewest clothes possible in order to stay warm and dry, and to pay for somewhere to live. This level of income he termed the *poverty line*.
(**From** *Revise GCSE Sociology*, S. Moore, Charles Letts & Co Ltd)

NOTES: *Poverty: absolute and relative*

A Absolute poverty: not having enough money to feed, clothe and house oneself adequately.
Poverty line: amount of income below which one can't feed, c. + h. oneself adequately. (J. Rowntree)

● WHY MAKE NOTES?

1 They help you revise. When you revise, you haven't time to reread **whole books**, but you can study **notes**.
2 They help you with projects and essays. Your notes present you with a summary of whatever was relevant in any publications you have read for your project or essay.
3 The actual process of making notes, the effort to think and express yourself, serves to fix the information in your mind.
4 It is always easier to remember your own words than someone else's.

● HOW TO GO ABOUT MAKING NOTES

Consider the following two scenarios in which students are to make notes on a text about the future of nuclear power. Which approach is the better?

Student one You are a conscientious worker and intend not to leave out anything important.

- you start reading on page one and concentrate on each sentence as you come to it.
- you make notes on three or four important points on page one.
- you read page two and note down several more important facts.
- you note that no new nuclear power stations have been ordered in the US since 1978.
- you note that nuclear power generates waste.
- you note details of actual and near nuclear accidents.
- at the end of the text you have, let us suppose, three A4 pages of notes.

Student two You, too, are conscientious, but adopt a totally different approach.

- first, you skim.
- you aim to find out:
    (a) what the writer's central point is
    (b) what his main supporting points are
- you read the first paragraph on page one.
- you read a few topic sentences on different pages.
- you read the last two paragraphs of the text.
- you think hard, striving to work out the gist of the text. What is the crucial message? How do all the other points contribute to it?
- you discover the central message: nuclear power has vast potential and should be increased.
- you establish that the supporting points are:
    – reactors can and should be made safe
    – waste disposal should be carried out safely
    – a world body should be set up to supervise the nuclear power industry
- you jot down the main and supporting points.
- you read the text more closely for further valuable points: figures, examples, etc.
- you then write out a neat set of notes, beginning with the main and supporting points.

Student one has not sought the central theme. Instead, by concentrating on each sentence as it comes, he or she risks becoming preoccupied with detail and failing to see the central point. Even if it is discovered:

- it may have taken too much time.
- unimportant details may have been unnecessarily noted: importance can only be judged in relation to the main point which must therefore, be established at an early stage.
- when he or she comes to reread the notes months later, the central point may not stand out clearly from the surrounding detail.

Student two, on the other hand, has focused clearly on the most important point:

- has judged every detail in the light of it.
- has had a proper basis for deciding what to note and what to omit.
- has so written the notes that key points are made to stand out.

● WHEN TO MAKE NOTES

1 From a book. Only make notes on a section of a book (e.g. a chapter) when you have **understood** what its main and supporting points are. This will be after you have first skimmed and jotted down the essential points and then reread the text more closely for important detail.

2 From a lesson/lecture. If you have to make your own notes when a person is talking or lecturing (not dictating), the same principle about first understanding the message applies. Listen and think until you are certain you have understood an idea before writing a note on it. Judging the right moment to make a note is a skill that it takes time to develop. It is important to achieve a suitable balance between time for listening and time for writing. As far as names, dates, figures, sums of money, etc, are concerned, you will have to note those down as you hear them. You may also note down at an early stage the structure of the talk if you are told it at the beginning.

For example, if the teacher says 'I am going to talk about the uses Eskimos make of snow and there are six of them', you can scribble down something like this at once: 'Eskimos' Uses of Snow (6)' and then look out for each use as it is described. You should listen for expressions which indicate that a new use is going to be mentioned, e.g. 'The next use of snow is as . . .', 'Another important way . . .', 'Again, . . .', 'An unexpected way in which . . .', 'Lastly, . . .'.

It is not easy while listening to a lecture to make a set of notes from which it will be easy to revise. You may have to regard what you jot down at the time as a *rough* set, which you will then rewrite as a *neat* set of notes. If you do decide to do this, it is important to write your neat notes within about 24 hours of the rough ones. Otherwise, you are liable to be unable to sort out any difficult or unclear aspects of your jottings.

● WHAT TO NOTE

Your notes will be a summary of the essential points of a text, or a summary of just those points that are relevant to a project or essay you are writing, (possibly the same as the essential points).

You may also note:

- important terms.
- definitions of those terms.
- important names, dates, figures, etc.

With the exception of (i) quotations and (ii) definitions, do not copy whole sentences from a text. 'Process' the information in your mind and write words of your own.

PRACTICE

Skim and then read the following text to work out its main points. Then look at the list of points that follows it. Write 'M' beside each main point and 'O' beside points that you would omit from a set of notes.

What is mountain biking? It's everything from quiet rides in the countryside to the fast and furious action of professional racing. You can ride along bridleways, canal towpaths or even city streets, and some riders take their mountain bikes (MTBs) on rugged expeditions to such demanding places as Scotland's highest peaks – two brothers once even rode their MTBs up 19 000 foot Mount Kilimanjaro, the tallest mountain in all of Africa.

You can go just about anywhere with an MTB, because they're like Land Rovers on two wheels. With their knobbly tyres and up to 21 gears, mountain bikes have the traction to tackle almost any trail. They're built tough, so you don't have to stick to the road, but that means they are also great for riding in town. No punctures, no worry.

Mountain bikes first got started in America ten years ago, when a group of Californians started racing down dirt roads on one-speed bikes with back-pedal brakes. Soon, they decided they needed a bike which could handle rough ground easily and safely.

Before long, these specially-built bikes became available in the United States, and about three years ago the new style caught on in Britain. Today, over half of all new bikes sold here are mountain bikes. So what is the explanation for this popularity? In a word – fun!

Partly because they can go anywhere and partly because they look so cool, you can't help having a good time with a mountain bike. Whether you pedal along easily on a flat trail, ride high in the mountains or enter a race, something about mountain bikes is good clean (or probably muddy!) fun.

What makes mountain bikes so special is their extra sturdy frames, wide tyres with deep tread, low gearing and motorcycle-style handlebars, for extra control while going downhill. Modern technology makes the bikes very lightweight – as little as 24 lbs for top race-models. Also, the gear shifting is foolproof, braking is better than ever and the best tyres stick to the trail like glue.

1 With a mountain bike (MTB) you can ride on level or rough ground, quietly or in stiff competition.
2 MTBs are tough: with deep-tread tyres and many gears they cope with most trails.
3 You can ride MTBs along canal towpaths and city streets.
4 Two brothers once rode their MTBs up 19 000 foot Mount Kilimanjaro.
5 MTBs started in the US and are now very popular in the UK.
6 MTBs are like Land Rovers on two wheels.
7 A group of Californians on one-speed bikes with back-pedal brakes started MTBs.
8 MTBs are liked because they are versatile, stylish and fun.
9 Riding on a mountain bike is often muddy.
10 Other special features of MTBs include very strong frames, light weight, and foolproof gear changing.

ADVANCED PRACTICE

Skim and then read this text to work out:

(a) its central message
(b) its main supporting points

Then look at the list of points that follows it. Write 'A' beside the central point, 'B' beside each main supporting point and 'O' against points you would omit from your notes.

Over the last decade, the profits to be made in the $150 billion pharmaceutical market have inspired a new form of forgery: drugs that are not what they seem. The names are familiar. They include Zantac, the world's best-selling ulcer drug; Selokeen, a Swedish-made cardiac drug; Adriamicin, for leukaemia; Fansidar, used against malaria. The counterfeits look like the real thing, right down to the labels, manufacturers' pamphlets and purity seals. In Africa, fakery is epidemic: pharmacists in Nigeria estimate that more than a quarter of all medicines on the market are phony or substandard. One, sold as an antibiotic, was 'nothing but talcum powder – perfume and all,' says Nigeria's Health Minister Olikoye Ransome-Kuti. The cost to legitimate manufacturers is staggering – the theft of 'intellectual property' worth billions of dollars. In a study published by the US International Trade Commission, American manufacturers estimated that counterfeiting in the States alone was costing them $16.2 million a year. The human cost is incalculable: 'Hundreds if not thousands of (Africans) have died,' says Susan Foster, a health economist at the London School of Hygiene and Tropical Medicine. 'This is a really nasty business.' Says John Dunne, director of drug management for the World Health Organization in Geneva: 'It's mass murder.'

Who are the counterfeiters? They range from bathtub chemists in South East Asia to high-tech manufacturers in countries like Argentina and Greece, working with chemicals freely available on the open market. Often the point of origin **is a** nation that does not recognize international drug patents – India, for example, or Thailand. From there a finished drug or its basic chemical components may be shipped **anywhere through a series of** cut-rate brokers who function as middlemen. Thai counterfeiters working from a mobile factory five years ago flooded the Burmese market with worthless copies of Hoffman-LaRoche's Fansidar and Wellcome's Septrin antibiotic. Hong Kong police have intercepted at least one shipment of Thai-made fakes bound for the United States according to a US congressional investigator. 'The trail for a drug found in Britain may be Brazil, Chile, Argentina, Spain, Italy,' says Paul Carratu, a partner with his father, Vincent, in a London investigative firm currently handling 60 counterfeiting cases. 'We've had cases covering six or seven countries, and the brokers have never checked the goods. Let's say they don't want to know.'

(From 'The Pill Pirates', T. Masland and R. Marshall, *Newsweek*, November 5, 1990)

1 The names of the forged drugs are well known.
2 The fake drugs and their packaging look like the real thing.
3 The making of fake drugs has increased enormously in the last 10 years.
4 There are forgeries of Zantac, the ulcer drug.
5 The faking represents a serious loss of money to the drug companies.
6 A drug in Nigeria, sold as an antibiotic, was only talcum powder.
7 Many people have died through taking fake drugs.
8 Hong Kong police intercepted Thai-made drugs bound for the US.
9 Fake drugs often originate in one country and are distributed through a succession of others to their final destination.
10 A London firm is currently investigating 60 cases of fake drugs.

● **HOW TO SET OUT NOTES**

If notes are to help you revise, they must be very clear and legible.
1 Indicate the source of the notes (title of book, author, page).
2 Sort out levels of organization within a text: indicate headings and subheadings very carefully. Distinguish between headings and points at one level and those at a lower level. Follow the divisions used in the book you are making notes on.

Look at the example of setting out notes shown below. Your notes might be set out like this, or you may wish to devise patterns of your own.

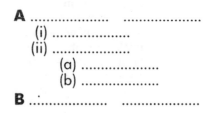

chapter headings in capitals

Chapter 8   EDUCATION

A ....

main sections within chapter

(i) ....
(ii) ....
   (a) ....
   (b) ....

B ....

subsections within a section	(i) ....
	(ii) ....
	(iii) ....
further subdivisions within a subsection	(a) ....
	(b) ....
	(c) ....

C ....

3 There are various ways of distinguishing the different levels of organization within a text:

(a) Capital letters, underlining. You could use capitals just for chapter headings; you could use underlining for main sections within a chapter.

(b) Indentation. This means starting each level slightly to the right of the level above it. In the example above, the Roman numerals (i), (ii), etc, are slightly to the right of **A**, **B**, **C**; and the small letters (a), (b), (c), are to the right of the Roman numerals. If you keep precisely to these positions on the page, your notes will be much clearer to you.

(c) Numbers and letters. Have a clear system of numbers and letters and **keep strictly to it**. A good idea is to keep Arabic numerals (1, 2, 3, 4, etc) for chapter headings; to use capital letters (A B C D) for the main sections inside a chapter; to use Roman numerals (i), (ii), (iii), (iv) for subsections within the main sections; and if any further subdivisions are needed, to use small letters ((a), (b), (c)). This way you (i) alternate numbers and letters and (ii) alternate types of letter and types of numeral, thus helping to avoid confusion.

● INDICATE RELATIONS BETWEEN POINTS

Below is an example of notes where the relationships between points are made to **stand out** clearly. This is important. Many exam questions ask for **causes**, **examples**, **ways**, **functions**, **differences** and so on. These words are to do with relationships. So if you include them in your notes where appropriate, it will help you with studying and revising for your exams.

One relationship in the text below is **contrast**, indicated by the word **but**.

1 What other relationships are indicated in the notes?
2 What words indicate their presence?
3 How are they made to stand out?

As large-scale fishing fleets deplete the fish populations on which dolphins feed, the animals are sometimes forced to move inshore in search of alternative food sources. Local, small-scale coastal fishermen, noticing a decline in fish catches, and at the same time seeing an apparent increase in dolphin numbers, may deduce that a growing dolphin population is eating ever larger amounts of fish, causing catches to diminish – a view which their governments (whose flawed fisheries – management policies are actually responsible for the fish stocks' decline) may well be keen to encourage. In such circumstances, the fishermen may feel compelled to kill dolphins to reduce competition for the depleted fish stocks.

The most famous example of this occurred off the village of Katsumoto, on Japan's Iki Island, between 1976 and 1982. When catches of yellowtail tuna fish in the area went into a serious decline, the region's fishermen blamed this on an increase in dolphin numbers and, by way of a solution, began driving large numbers of dolphins into the bays and killing them.

Many scientists argued that the fisheries' decline was more likely caused by a combination of factors: the effects of large-net fisheries from Korea and other regions of Japan (together, possibly, with pollution off the coast) and the

occurrence of a natural, though unusual, warm ocean current which began flowing through the area in the 1970s, displacing the colder, more nutrient-rich waters in the region. Despite such arguments, the villagers killed a total of about 6000 bottle-nosed dolphins, Risso's dolphins, Pacific white-sided dolphins and false killer whales. The mass slaughter ended in 1982, when the dolphins stopped appearing in such large numbers around the yellowtails' breeding grounds.
(From 'Flipper's Dilemma', K. Mulvaney, *BBC Wildlife*, September 1990)

Notes stating clearly the relationships between points:

Why fishermen attack dolphins

Reason:
Fishermen <u>first</u> reduce fish stocks ∴ dolphins move inshore for food.
<u>next</u> see more dolphins and fewer fish inshore and blame d. for fewer fish ∴ kill dolphins.

Example: Katsumoto villagers in Japan kill many d. 1976 - 1982.

But Scientists say two factors probably caused fish decline:
Cause 1. Korean and Japanese large-net fisheries
Cause 2. Warm current takes place of cold nutrient-rich current

● USE DIAGRAMS SOMETIMES

The advantages of using diagrams are twofold:

1 They have a strong visual impact which greatly helps you to remember their content.

2 The process of designing a suitable diagram really forces you to come to grips with the text and makes you understand it.

Below is an example of a text on which notes have been made in diagrammatic form. Studying this example should give you a good idea of how to approach your own work using diagrams.

One very famous study of the relationship between the media and youth was done in the 1960s by Stanley Cohen, who studied 'mods' and 'rockers'. He found that the mass media helped to create the fashion of mods and rockers, and then constructed stories which created a stereotype of these two groups as violent rivals, always fighting. This led to young people identifying themselves as mods or rockers, seeing violence as appropriate behaviour to adopt, and going out to fight each other. The police in turn had a stereotyped image of every person who dressed in the fashions of mod or rocker and assumed they were out looking for trouble, and tended to treat them accordingly. Had there been less sensationalization in the papers, there may not have been as much trouble.
(From *Revise GCSE Sociology*, S. Moore, Charles Letts & Co Ltd)

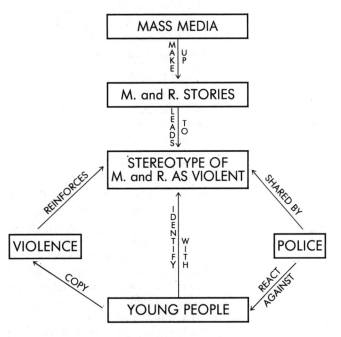

● USE I.E., E.G., AND SO ON

Use abbreviations sometimes: they save time and space. But do so prudently. Here are some common ones:

i.e. (that is): for expressing an idea *in other words*
e.g.: to introduce an example
∴: 'therefore', to precede a conclusion
= : between two ideas that mean the same
≠ : between two opposites

You can abbreviate any important word that occurs several times in your text. But do write out in full the first occurrence of it. Otherwise you might forget what your abbreviation stands for. Once you have started using a letter or group of letters as an abbreviation, always keep the same letter or letters for one idea. Don't use 'ch' to stand for 'chemical' in one place and 'c' for it in another, for example.

● BE ACCURATE

When making notes accuracy is very important. Record strictly what the text (or lecturer) says even if you disagree with it. Don't slip in your own views unless you make it absolutely clear that that is what you are doing. One way of doing this is to put your own views on a separate line that starts with your initials, for example: J.I.R.D: . . . . Then, when you reread your notes, you can distinguish your ideas from the author's.

● ORGANIZE YOUR NOTES

One large ring binder may be enough for all your notes. If so, divide it up according to the subjects you are studying. Have a method of quickly finding where, for example, your chemistry notes are or where your geography notes are. You can buy index sheets or subject dividers with letters down the right hand edge to indicate where each section is. If you use a ring binder and A4 file paper for all your notes, you can easily slip in a new page of notes wherever it fits in. Whenever you make notes, do file them immediately so that they do not get lost. If you do not organize your notes well, but carelessly put them in an inappropriate place, then the information on them is **as good as lost**. Information which you can't find is useless.

89

Read the following text and compare the two sets of notes on it. What faults can you find in one of the sets of notes?

Chapter 8 Education

There is a clear distinction between formal and informal learning.

Formal learning

This is the type of academic or practical learning that people are taught in **schools** and colleges. It consists of clearly defined skills taught in lessons in such a way that they can be graded through examinations, for example, maths. Formal learning is the type of learning that is supposed to take place at school.

Informal learning

This form of learning is part of the general socialization process, through which we learn to be normal members of society. Informal learning is not organized or examined, and it is learnt through casual, daily contact with other people around us. The most important people are the family and the peer group (people of our own age), and also teachers.

In modern, complex societies such as our own, much of the learning process takes place in schools through formal learning. In most societies throughout history learning has been informal, through casual contact, each generation passing on its knowledge to the next.

Even in schools, much of what we learn is through informal learning. Although teachers may officially be teaching a particular subject, for example, English Language, in fact they may also be teaching attitudes and skills which are no part of English. In order to teach a certain point, the teacher may get the pupils to read something on life in a factory. The pupils are not just learning English, they are also learning about work and developing attitudes to it.

The hidden curriculum

This unofficial learning is known as the 'hidden curriculum' and is learnt from teachers and also from the peer group. It is called the hidden curriculum because the correct term for the subjects we learn at school is the 'curriculum', and the informal learning is hidden within this. Gradually expectations and ideas are learned through contact with others at school.

Examples of this hidden curriculum are:

1 **Gender roles** Teachers act differently to boys and girls (although they may not realize this) and help to develop different attitudes and patterns of behaviour between them.

2 **Racial attitudes** Like gender differences, pupils become aware of differences in ethnic groups, through the attitudes of teachers and other pupils, and the content of textbooks.

3 **Social class differences** The importance of social class and its relationship to such things as income, the way people speak, differences in housing and possibly clothing can all be found at school. There is some evidence that teachers prefer middle-class children and are more sympathetic to them.

4 **Social control and preparation for work** Apart from actual subjects taught at school, pupils also learn to be obedient and they are encouraged to work hard. This prepares them for work later in life.

The peer group

People with whom we identify and whose behaviour we copy are known as the peer group. At school, this is usually the other pupils with whom we are friendly (or whom we admire). The peer group is extremely important in understanding pupils' behaviour. In lower streams, the pupils will be more likely to 'muck around' and pupils who are attentive and hard working will be the object of jokes and will be outsiders. This places pressure on pupils not to work hard. The opposite is true in the higher streams.

One study, by Willis, showed that by 'mucking about' at school, the pupils in lower streams coped with what they saw as irrelevant and boring; they also ensured their own failure. However, the very mucking about was just the skill they needed to cope with the boring jobs that they would eventually get. In short, the pupils prepared themselves to cope with boring jobs, without realizing it.

(From *Keyfacts GCSE Sociology*, S. Moore, Charles Letts & Co Ltd)

SET OF NOTES A

Chapter 8   Education

A. <u>Formal Learning</u>

Specific skills learned in lessons, followed by exams. What we are <u>supposed</u> to learn at school.

B. <u>Informal Learning</u>

Attitudes, skills picked up incidentally from people around us, not timetabled. This way we learn to be members of society and other things, often through subjects like English.

C. <u>Hidden Curriculum</u>

Things learnt informally at school, not stated in any syllabus. E.g.
- (i) <u>Gender roles</u>: ways boys/girls expected to behave
- (ii) <u>Racial attitudes</u>: pupils learn ethnic differences
- (iii) <u>Social class differences</u>: in income, speech, housing, clothes
- (iv) <u>Social control</u> and <u>preparation for work</u>: obedience + hard work, useful for later work

D. <u>Peer Group</u>

Other pupils with whom we identify and copy.
In <u>lower streams</u> pupils 'muck about'. Hard workers mocked.
In <u>higher streams</u> other way round.
<u>Mucking about</u> may prepare lower streams for coping with boring jobs.

SET OF NOTES B

8   Education

1. <u>Formal L</u>

This is the type of academic or practical learning that people are taught in schools and colleges. Formal learning is the type of learning that is supposed to take place in school.

2. <u>Informal learning</u>

General socialization for normal members of soc. Not. org. or ex. In English we often learn about life in factories.

3. <u>Hidden C.</u>

Unofficial learning, not on the curriculum i.e.

1. <u>Gender roles</u>

Teachers shouldn't treat boys and girls differently.

2. Racism

Pupils learn to be racists at school. Pupils also learn about social class at school. Income is important. Teachers always prefer middle-class children.

3. Peer groups

We usually get on with other people of our own age. Mucking about is important. It enables us to prepare for our future boring jobs.

Now some practice in making notes

Imagine that you are writing a project about the environmental impact of cars and you will include a section on the effects of fast driving. In the course of your reading, you come across the text below. Read it and make notes on it to help you with your project. Remember to put into effect all the advice and tips about making good notes that you have learnt in this chapter. A sample answer is given at the end of this section.

Slowing down to reduce pollution

There are now 350 million cars in use worldwide and together they produce about 10 000 billion cubic metres of exhaust fumes every year. It has been calculated that the fumes from West Germany's 25 million motor vehicles alone would cover the entire country with a layer of poisonous fumes two metres high. This would suffocate all life, if it were not for the fact that much of it is carried up into the atmosphere.

If you drive at high speed, the output of exhaust gas greatly increases. Nitrogen oxides, which are strongly suspected of being culprits in tree damage, are produced at twice the rate in a given distance from a car travelling at 100 mph compared with one travelling at 55 mph. The output of other poisons such as carbon monoxide and hydro-carbons also rises sharply and so does petrol consumption.

In addition, there is the risk to personal health. Where there are no speed restrictions, accident statistics read like a medical bulletin during an epidemic. In Germany there was a total of 179 000 car crashes in 1984 in which over 10 000 people died. Of the whole population, one person in a hundred was injured within that 12 months.

Speed limits on motorways – although they are often broken – reduce the figures dramatically. In 1974 a 55 mph speed limit was introduced in the US. There were over 55 000 road fatalities the preceding year when the motorway speed limit was 65 mph. Ten years later this figure has dropped to 44 000 despite a doubling of the traffic volume.

Reducing your driving speed is the simplest way of reducing pollution, conserving fuel, and surviving to drive another day.

(From *Blueprint for a Green Planet*, J. Seymour and H. Girardet, Dorling Kindersley)

ANSWERS
Practice on page 84
Main points: 1, 2, 5, 8, 10. Other points would be omitted from notes.
Advanced practice on page 85
1 'O', 2 'B', 3 'A', 4 'O', 5 'B', 6 'O', 7 'B', 8 'O', 9 'B', 10 'O'.
Practice on page 90
All the faults are to be found in set B. 1 Omission of 'Chapter' from heading.

2 Because only Arabic numerals are used, there is confusion in the organization of the points.

3 Tendency to use full sentences: should reduce words to a minimum.

4 First sentence of the text is copied out in full – not processed.

5 The word 'learning' is abbreviated to L. in the first subheading. It is not appropriate to abbreviate this **first** use of an important word.

6 The note-maker might not understand his abbreviations 'org.' and 'ex.' at a later date.

7 Learning about factories is a detail which should be omitted; 'often' is wrong information.

8 Omission of the important information that informal learning is from people around us.

9 The note-maker's abbreviation 'C' after 'Hidden' may not be understood later.

10 'i.e.' is wrong: should be 'e.g.'

11 The point under 'Gender roles' is missed: that pupils **learn from teachers' behaviour**.

12 The point under 'Racism' is incorrect.

13 The heading 'Social class differences' is omitted.

14 Information on social class needn't be given in full sentences; speech, housing and clothes are omitted; 'always prefer' is a gross distortion of 'There is some evidence that . . .'; the point about teachers' preferences should be omitted.

15 The important definition of 'peer group' is omitted; 'mucking about' is given undue importance: the notes wrongly imply that it has a useful role for **all** future jobs.

Specimen notes on text on car speed on page 92

Car speed should be reduced

    Notes on p.160 of 'Blueprint for a Green Planet' by J. Seymour and H. Girardet, Dorling Kindersley.

Car exhausts already produce vast volumes of toxic gases.
Speed should be reduced.
Reasons: at high speed:
    1. much more gas given off per mile travelled.
    2.   "   " petrol used   "   "   "
    3. many more accidents.
      E.g. lowering sp. limits in US reduced accidents.

Chapter 11
Writing skills 1

THE PURPOSE OF THIS CHAPTER

This chapter deals with the following writing skills:

- Limiting the topic
- Gathering material
- Structure of a fairly long piece of writing
- Relevance and unity
- Concise writing
- Argument

Its purpose is to show you the importance of good writing skills as an aid to studying, and how best to develop your own skills.

Some of the skills explained in this and the next chapter are more applicable to work of essay or project length, e.g. the structure of a piece of writing. Others, such as relevance, apply to every sentence that you write.

● LIMITING THE TOPIC

For some pieces of writing you are given a broad subject and asked to choose a specific topic within it. For example, you may be asked to write on 'The motor car and the environment'. You would need to decide which aspects to discuss. Such an assignment is not to be seen as an opportunity to write all you know on the subject as a whole. Within the subject you could consider these more specific topics:

(a) ways in which cars pollute the environment
(b) future improvements in car design and types of fuel
(c) government policy on transport in the light of the car's polluting effects
(d) public transport as a way of reducing the environmental effects of the internal combustion engine
(e) the future without the car

PRACTICE

Narrow down the following broad subjects into possible essay topics:

1 Global warming.
2 Tropical rain forests.
3 A subject in English, history, science or any of your examination subjects that require written work.

● GATHERING MATERIAL

1 **Look for** books which may have a chapter on your topic. Hunt through tables of contents. Look for articles in journals, magazines and newspapers.

2 Look out for radio and TV programmes, especially if your subject is topical.

3 Ask for assistance and information at school and in public libraries.

94

4 Make notes on relevant parts of the books and articles you find.

5 Continually refer back to your topic to **check** the relevance of the notes you are making.

6 As you read, **jot down** ideas for your assignment on a separate piece of paper, not on your notes.

PRACTICE

Which of these publications would be likely to include materials useful to an essay entitled 'What can be done to reduce the harmful effects of the car on the environment?'.

1 'Britain's Transport Crisis'.

2 'Blueprint for a Green Planet'.

3 'The Car in the Future'.

4 'The Complete Book of Self-Sufficiency'.

5 'Moving Britain into the 1990s' (Labour Party transport policy document).

6 'Ford Escort Owner's Manual'.

7 'Hydrogen: the fuel of the future'.

● STRUCTURE OF A FAIRLY LONG PIECE OF WRITING

You can make a plan only when you have made notes on useful chapters and articles, thought hard about the subject and decided on a topic and your view on it.

Let us suppose you have chosen this title: 'The immediate and longer term future of the car.' You take the view that for the next 30 years or so everything must be done to reduce car pollution by improving car design and fuels and developing public transport. After that there should be a pollution-free car but with controls on numbers and continued emphasis on public transport.

The usual structure for an essay, a project, a report or any fairly long piece of writing is in three parts:

1 Introduction.

2 Main body.

3 Conclusion.

1 Introduction This prepares the reader for the main body of your account. You can do this in several ways:

● by stating the background or situation that has given rise to your topic. In this case you could mention the obvious benefits of the car and its drawbacks. You could mention the increasing number of cars.
● by defining the scope of your topic. In this case, how far into the future you are looking.
● by defining terms which have a broad meaning. In a discussion of vegeterian diets, for example, you would define **vegetarian**; in writing about deserts, you might need to explain and define what is and what is not a desert as far as your account is concerned.
● by identifying the important issue or issues and how you will deal with them.
● by indicating any particular problems.
● by making an apt quotation.

- by referring briefly to your own views or conclusion on the main issue.
- by outlining the main divisions of the body of your assignment.

Background

Define terms

Scope

Identify issues

Problems

Introduction

Sum up conclusions

Apt quotation

Outline divisions

Very few introductions would include all these points. Do not make your introductions too long. You may combine elements from more than one of the above items.

PRACTICE

Write an introduction to a piece of writing on the topic 'The immediate and longer term future of the car.'

2 **Main body** This is where you present your account of the topic. Do it in a logical order which is clear to your reader. Here is an approach to organizing an extensive description:

Think of your material as consisting of several **aspects** and describe one aspect at a time. List all the aspects at the outset and then deal with them in the order you have listed them. The order you choose must have a basis, e.g.:

(a) most important first, then next most important
(b) from large to small (when describing something physical)
(c) outside then inside

If you need to include stretches of narrative, work out how best to fit them into your overall plan. If you have to present an argument, work out how you will arrange your evidence and where you will deal with opposing points (see the section on 'Argument', p. 99).

Whatever organization you choose, try to have a **natural progression** from one point to the next.

3 Conclusion

- bring together the main points of your account. State them in summary form.
- state the results of your thinking, your conclusions on the issues you have discussed.
- avoid introducing new ideas.

PRACTICE

Make a plan for the main body and conclusion of a piece of writing either on a topic of your own choice or on 'The immediate and longer term future of the car.'

● RELEVANCE AND UNITY

Teachers and examiners frequently complain that students write irrelevant material. This can arise through not reading questions carefully enough and not referring back to the question from time to time as you write. The problem applies to all subjects.

A piece of writing should have unity. That is, it should have one theme and every point mentioned should be related to that theme.

PRACTICE

Try this exercise. Given the title 'The future of the motor car in the light of its impact on the environment', which of these points are relevant?

1 Direct fuel injection (less fuel used).

2 Ceramic engine parts.

3 Battery technology.

4 Diesel lorries.

5 Commuters.

6 The amount of energy and resources used in car manufacture.

7 Improvements in car safety.

8 New road construction.

9 Measures to encourage bicycle use.

10 Car insurance.

11 The amount of land needed to produce ethanol.

12 Improvement in rail travel.

13 Gadgets like carphones and fax machines in cars.

14 Hydrogen as a fuel.

15 Sports car design.

16 Passenger comfort.

17 Two-stroke petrol engines.

18 Taxation to discourage car use.

19 Traffic congestion.

20 Total abolition of the car.

When answering questions, follow instructions. Where you are asked for a **description** of an experiment, **describe** it; where you are asked for the **results** of an experiment, give the **results**. Restrict your answer to what is relevant to the question.

PRACTICE

Below is a plan for a piece of writing on 'Household waste and energy conservation'. Strike out any points in it that you think are irrelevant.

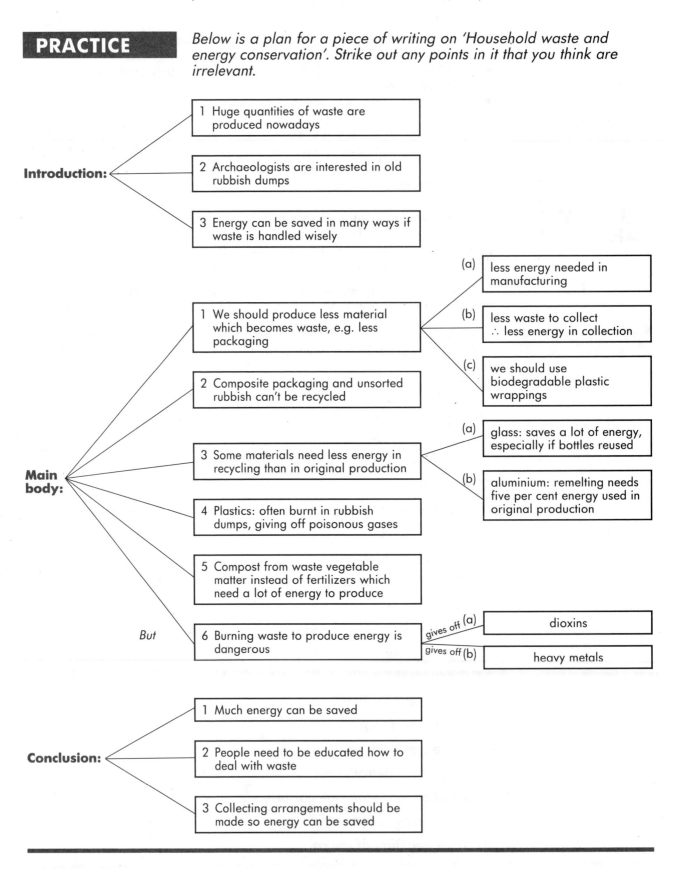

Introduction:

1 Huge quantities of waste are produced nowadays

2 Archaeologists are interested in old rubbish dumps

3 Energy can be saved in many ways if waste is handled wisely

Main body:

1 We should produce less material which becomes waste, e.g. less packaging

(a) less energy needed in manufacturing

(b) less waste to collect ∴ less energy in collection

(c) we should use biodegradable plastic wrappings

2 Composite packaging and unsorted rubbish can't be recycled

3 Some materials need less energy in recycling than in original production

(a) glass: saves a lot of energy, especially if bottles reused

(b) aluminium: remelting needs five per cent energy used in original production

4 Plastics: often burnt in rubbish dumps, giving off poisonous gases

5 Compost from waste vegetable matter instead of fertilizers which need a lot of energy to produce

But 6 Burning waste to produce energy is dangerous

gives off (a) dioxins

gives off (b) heavy metals

Conclusion:

1 Much energy can be saved

2 People need to be educated how to deal with waste

3 Collecting arrangements should be made so energy can be saved

● **CONCISE WRITING**

It is sometimes necessary to get down the maximum information in the minimum space. These are some techniques:

1 **Question:** keep strictly to the terms of the question.

2 **Ideas:** work out your key ideas and reject others.

3 **Words:** work out the fewest number of words needed to state your point. Before writing, consider alternative ways of wording it.

4 **Repetition:** avoid repeating ideas and words.

5 **List:** list points (but not in vertical columns) where appropriate. For example, see the sentence beginning 'Every Moslem . . .' under **colons** below.

6 **Colons:** colons can introduce a contrast, an explanation, or a set of detailed points, e.g.:
contrast – 'Napoleon did not defeat the Russians: winter defeated him.'
explanation – 'I did not enjoy the concert: the seats were too hard.'
details – 'Every Moslem must pray five times a day: at dawn, after midday, before sunset, just after sunset and during the early part of the night.'

7 **Apposition:** use commas for words in apposition, e.g. 'In 1876 Otto, a German engineer, made an internal combustion engine.' This is shorter than 'who was a German engineer'.

8 **Summarize:** where appropriate, use one general statement instead of several details, e.g. 'Every Moslem has five religious duties', instead of 'Every Moslem must recite their creed, pray five times a day, give money to the poor, fast during the month of Ramadan and make a pilgrimage to Mecca'.

PRACTICE

Study one paragraph which you have recently written. Rewrite it using fewer words.

● **ARGUMENT**

When you include argument in a piece of writing, bear these key elements in mind:

● there is an issue, a central point, a question.
● there are at least two points of view on the issue.
● you will adopt one point of view (do not try to hold two conflicting points of view).
● there are arguments for and against your point of view.
● there are arguments for and against other points of view.

What you must do:
1 Decide what the issue is – e.g. 'Should this country reintroduce the death penalty?'

2 Decide on your point of view. Sometimes this is difficult, especially when there are strong arguments on both sides. In the end you must decide where, on balance, you stand on the issue.

PRACTICE

For two or three of the topics that follow, do the following:

1 Decide what the issue is (there may be several possibilities).

2 Decide what your point of view would be.

*3 Think of two arguments **for** your point of view and two **against** it.*

A Smoking
B Privatization of government-owned organizations
C Gambling
D Selling weapons to other countries
E Being in debt
F Violence on television

Present your arguments in pairs or groups. For example:

One paragraph:

1 Those in favour of death penalty must establish that the state has the right to take life.
2 A state or person can only kill in self-defence and when no other option is available.
but 3 Other options (e.g. life imprisonment)are available.
therefore 4 State has no right to kill as a response to murder.

Another paragraph:

1 Some argue that capital punishment is a deterrent.
but 2 Statistics in America show that just as many murders occur in states that have the death penalty as in those without it.
3 A man who killed a policeman then shot himself: not deterred by prospect of death.
4 Many murderers may not reflect on consequences.
5 Life imprisonment may deter more than death penalty.

Remember that you must mention the most important arguments **against** your point of view. You can't ignore them. Your task is to show that each is either wrong or weaker than an opposing argument on your side.

It is a good approach to begin a paragraph with an argument opposed to your own and then shoot this opposing argument down in flames, ending with a strong assertion of an argument on your side. This is the approach used in the following paragraph about the deterrent effect of capital punishment. Study it!

One important argument in favour of capital punishment is that it deters other potential murderers. This sounds plausible at first. However, statistics show that there are just as many murders in American states with capital punishment in force as in those without it. Furthermore, information from Amnesty International states that 'Most politicians and certainly everybody connected with law enforcement and criminology acknowledge that there is no evidence to support the effectiveness of the death penalty as a better deterrent than imprisonment'. A recent incident in England further supports this point: a criminal who had murdered a policeman then shot himself. Clearly the prospect of death would not have influenced such a person. Again, to argue that the prospect of the death penalty deters is to make the assumption, wrongly, that criminals reflect before they murder. Very often they do not do so and often assume that they will never be caught. To many, the prospect of life imprisonment is more of a deterrent than death. Some, in fact, would even seek the publicity that goes with the death penalty. As far as terrorists are concerned, the death penalty is martyrdom and each martyr is an enormous asset to the terrorist's cause. Therefore the death penalty is not an effective deterrent. And would it ever be just to kill one person to deter another?

Argument may not take up the whole of a piece of writing. It may be included between sections of narrative, description, in a set of consequences, and so on.

Consider a new topic: the shipping of toxic waste between countries for disposal. Do the following:

1 **Read** 'The Times' article shown below. In addition, read more about this subject if you can find information on it.

2 Decide what the **issue** is.

3 Decide on your **point of view**.

4 Consider the **arguments** that are listed on page 102. Add arguments of your own, too, if you wish.

5 **Plan** an argument essay.

6 **Write** it.

<u>Michael McCarthy</u> on the dilemma Britain faces over toxic waste

When green turns to grey

Mrs Virginia Bottomley, Under-Secretary of State at the Department of the Environment, may have cause to thank the Mersey Docks and Harbour Company for its announcement on Wednesday that it would not handle 15 shipments of Canadian toxic waste. These hazardous cargoes, due to start arriving at the port next week, could not fail to provide environmentalists with ammunition for their campaign against such imports. Now the shipments may well have to return to Canada untreated.

Yet there are arguments in favour of allowing other countries' toxic waste to be imported into this country for destruction. Hazardous chemicals like polychlorinated biphenyls (PCBs) must be safely treated somewhere. Most countries do not have the facilities to do so; Britain does, and by offering to share them we are performing a service to the rest of the world.

Even environmentalists are divided on the issue. Greenpeace has set its face against all toxic waste imports, but Tom Burke, director of the Green Alliance, would rather see dangerous chemicals disposed of properly in Britain than inefficiently in the Third World. PCBs were used as transformer coolants all over the globe before their toxicity was recognized and they were banned.

(From *The Times*, August 11, 1989)

Government policy at present is to allow the import of toxic waste under stringent conditions. The reprocessing industry has grown fast in response to world demand, and is highly profitable. Rechem, the company operating the high-temperature incinerator in Pontypool, which was the ultimate destination of the Canadian waste, nearly doubled its pre-tax profits to £8.7m on a turnover of £19.5m, in the year to March. "Such bumper profits must make the business look attractive to other companies," commented *Investors Chronicle*.

But if companies like Rechem have won over the City, they will find it much tougher to win over the public. While it is generally accepted that our own waste must be dealt with, it is more difficult to convince people that taking in other countries' toxic waste is a good idea.

It is doubtful that the public will be reassured that Her Majesty's Inspectorate of Pollution will permit only properly regulated, documented and sealed cargoes of waste to enter; or that British technology can deal safely with chemicals like PCBs, or that chemical by-products of their destruction, such as dioxins, may not be the hazard they once were thought.

Growing local opposition to the Rechem plant has developed into a determined campaign to stop the consignment of Canadian waste which was due next week. Some protestors have threatened to block the lorries when they arrive at the incinerator gates, no doubt with the media in attendance. So Mrs Bottomley (who is minding the shop at the Environment Department in the absence of Christopher Patten and David Trippier) has reason to be grateful to the port authority for refusing to handle the cargoes.

It is an issue she has dealt with before. A year ago, as the newly appointed junior minister, she was faced with the affair of Karin B, the West German freighter carrying uncatalogued and unlicensed Italian waste that tried to sneak its cargo into Britain. In that case she was widely praised for turning away the ship.

Mrs Bottomley could hardly take the same action with the 15 shipments of Canadian PCBs that Rechem wishes to bring to Pontypool, properly catalogued, sealed, documented and authorized by the pollution inspectorate in accordance with government policy.

However, the distinction between Karin B and the Canadian cargoes may be lost on the public and the port authorities. On Tuesday night the port of Tilbury refused to handle a cargo of Canadian waste that had been fully authorized

by the inspectorate. Sir Bernard Braine, Conservative MP for Castle Point, an Essex constituency bordering the Thames, called the handling of toxic waste in the area scandalous, no doubt echoing the sentiments of his constituents.

National waste management practice as a whole is under review and will be tightened considerably in the forthcoming Green Bill. The Government has already made clear its opposition to the importation of waste for landfill – dumping on refuse sites. But so far it sees no reason to ban the import of hazardous waste for specialized destruction in high-technology facilities.

If the Rechem shipments did arrive, and were met with determined public opposition, the political price of continuing to defend toxic waste imports could prove too high. So while the constitutionalist in Mrs Bottomley will doubtless register stern disapproval of a port management deciding import policy, and a public company being prevented from going about its lawful business, it would be surprising if the practical politician in her did not offer silent thanks.

101

Arguments concerning toxic waste shipment

Study these arguments. Decide whether each is in favour of shipment or against it.

1 Very often a technologically advanced country has the means for safe disposal of toxic waste, whereas another country, e.g. a Third World one, may not.

2 By accepting cargoes from abroad we prevent the improper disposal of toxic waste either on land or at sea.

3 However suitable the incineration or other disposal process, there is always the possibility of an accident with potentially disastrous consequences.

4 By accepting toxic waste from abroad, a country in effect discourages the exporting country from developing industrial processes that produce little, if any, waste.

5 Environmental issues should be seen as global issues. So the question of where toxic waste originates and where it ends up are not so important.

6 Even those who claim the disposal processes are safe and efficient only claim a 99.99 per cent efficiency. This leaves unanswered the question of how damaging is the escape of 0.01 per cent of the toxic waste.

7 The trade in toxic waste is very big (one shipment every five minutes in 1985). It must be reduced or stopped. Otherwise waste-production is encouraged.

8 Refusing to handle toxic waste from abroad won't necessarily encourage other countries not to produce it in the first place. In the case of PCBs, for example, the chemical is no longer made. The need is to dispose safely of what used to be made, but is no longer made.

9 Waste-senders cheat and include undeclared toxic chemicals with other waste. The whole trade should be stopped.

10 The fact that waste-senders cheat is an argument **not** for ending the trade, but for ending the cheating by having proper regulation and inspection.

ANSWERS

Practice on page 95
1 Probably useful. 2 Probably useful. 3 Probably useful.
4 Unlikely to be useful. 5 Probably useful.
6 Unlikely to be useful. 7 Probably useful.

Practice on page 97
1 R (Relevant). 2 R. 3 R. 4 I (Irrelevant). 5 R. 6 R.
7 I. 8 R. 9 R. 10 I. 11 R. 12 R. 13 I. 14 R.
15 I. 16 I. 17 R. 18 R. 19 R. 20 R.

Practice on page 98
Irrelevant points: 'Archaeologists are interested in old rubbish dumps'.
'Plastics: often burnt in rubbish dumps, giving off poisonous gases'.

Practice on page 101
Arguments concerning toxic waste shipment.
Points in favour of it: 1, 2, 5, 8, 10.
Points against it: 3, 4, 6, 7, 9.

Chapter 12
Writing skills 2

THE PURPOSE OF THIS CHAPTER

This chapter continues the work of the previous chapter. It introduces you to these further skills of good writing:

- Combining information from several sources
- Proportion
- Evidence
- Unity at paragraph level
- First and second drafts
- Proof reading

In addition to developing these skills, get used to limiting the time allowed for written work in order to be ready for examination time restrictions.

● **COMBINING INFORMATION FROM SEVERAL SOURCES**

You can only do this successfully after first:

1 Reading through your notes.
2 Thinking out the subject and deciding your views.
3 Establishing **your own** framework of ideas, the set of headings under which you will present the topic.

For example, you want to examine the electric car as **pollution-free** and **practical** (your 'headings'). While considering the question of the car's pollution,

(a) you **read** L. Halstead's assessment in 'What the Experts Say' (see notes A on page 108)

(b) you **notice** 'charged from power-stations ∴ only replacing one form of pollution with another'

(c) you **think** 'No mention of **other** environmentally friendly sources of electricity'

so (d) you **check** notes on *Blueprint for a Green Planet* (see notes B on page 109) and **see** '–need renewable electricity source' (under 'Other fuels', point 4)

(e) you **check** notes E on 'Watt Car' (page 110) and **notice** the reference to **solar** power in California

(f) you **take** these sources together with a reading of 'Powered by Hydrogen' (notes C on page 110) and **conclude** that L. Halstead's objection 'replacing one form of pollution with another' could fall away with the development of a renewable source of energy such as solar energy.

You have combined ideas from several sources.

Under the heading **practicality**, you consider the batteries. L. Halstead states the need to improve battery technology. Is there evidence of this in other sources? Reach your own conclusion after:

(a) comparing Peugeot's *Vert* car and GM's *Impact* (in 'Electric Cars on Trial') (see notes D on page 110)

and (b) considering what GM's engineers are doing for battery life (in 'Watt Car')

When combining information from several sources:

1 Don't **repeat** ideas.

2 Don't include **contradictory** ideas. Try to resolve conflicting accounts. If writers differ, ask yourself **why**. What further information could settle the matter?

Information from several sources

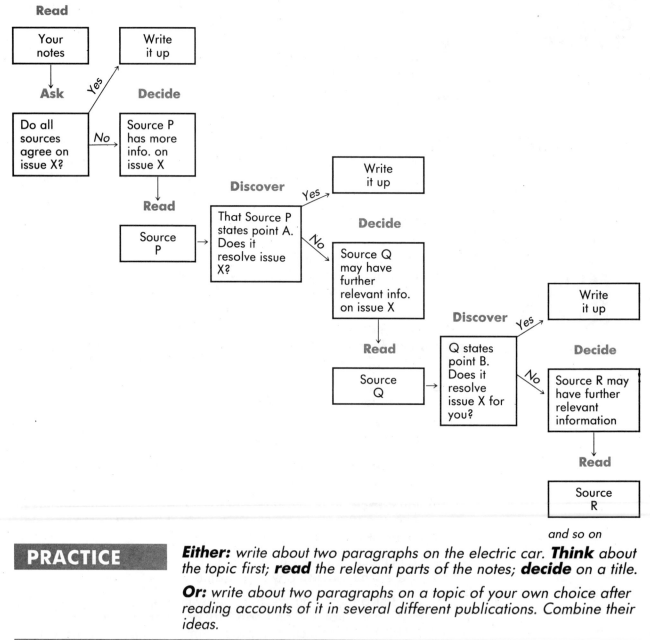

and so on

PRACTICE

Either: write about two paragraphs on the electric car. **Think** about the topic first; **read** the relevant parts of the notes; **decide** on a title.

Or: write about two paragraphs on a topic of your own choice after reading accounts of it in several different publications. Combine their ideas.

● **PROPORTION**

In any piece of writing you must consider carefully how much to write on each aspect of your topic. Your decision will depend largely on the **importance** of each aspect. The completed account should appear balanced, with the right proportion of space given to each section. Avoid writing excessively on an aspect just because you have found a book which goes into it in great detail.

1 *In an assignment on the future of the car, which of the proportions given below would you consider appropriate and which inappropriate? Refer to the notes on pages 108 to 110 to help you decide.*

1 Three paragraphs on lean-burn engines, one on improved public transport.

2 One paragraph on ethanol as a fuel, one on methanol.

3 Three paragraphs on electric cars, three sentences on hydrogen cars.

4 Two paragraphs on battery technology, one on alternative fuels to petrol.

2 *Choose a topic on which you have to write, list the various aspects of it and decide roughly how many paragraphs to devote to each.*

EVIDENCE

The other common failing (and the usual cause of unusually low marks) is lack of detailed information to support arguments.

(From the Report on the June 1988 A level History examinations, Cambridge University Local Examinations Syndicate)

The examiners go on to make these points about the need for evidence:

- without evidence, analysis is superficial and not convincing.
- however, there is no need to **go into detail** when mentioning events or policies as evidence: it is enough just to **refer to** a good example.
- using a **variety** of examples will earn you marks.
- thorough preparation of a **whole** topic is necessary to answer a question on **part** of the topic, even though you will not mention all the detail directly in your writing.

Provide one or two examples or pieces of evidence to support each of these points:

1 Some dogs are too dangerous for members of the public to keep at home.

2 Politicians sometimes break their promises.

3 Most prisons are 'universities of crime'. Their character should be radically changed to educate prisoners away from crime.

4 Health education should be part of the school curriculum.

5 Personal qualities are just as important for one's career as academic qualifications.

UNITY AT PARAGRAPH LEVEL

A paragraph should have one controlling idea. Every sentence in the paragraph should support that idea in some way. Often, the first sentence is a topic sentence that states the controlling idea. For example:

Although the forests that cover the mountain slopes of Switzerland are a delight to look at, they also perform a crucial task. They protect the villages, farms and roads in the valleys below from avalanches and landslides. It has been estimated that it would cost the country billions of pounds to build barriers along roads and around villages if the 'free' protective function of the mountain forests were to fail. As a result of forest die-back, that is fast becoming a possibility.

} Forests perform a task (topic)

} Their task: protect against avalanches

} Alternatives, if trees fail, are expensive

} They may be needed, as trees are failing

All connected with the tasks of forests

(From *Blueprint for a Green Planet*, J. Seymour and H. Girardet, Dorling Kindersley)

PRACTICE

Which sentences in each of the following paragraphs do not contribute to its controlling idea?

1 *1* When the price of petrol was very high, the Brazilian government decided to make ethanol from sugar cane and use it as an alternative to petrol. *2* Ethanol is a form of alcohol. *3* It is the type that occurs in alcoholic drinks. *4* Rum is another alcoholic liquid that can be produced from sugar cane. *5* Brazil had the necessary huge land area to produce ethanol, which was satisfactory as a fuel. *6* However, it was more expensive than petrol. *7* So although 95 per cent of Brazilians used it at first, less than 50 per cent do so now. *8* In Holland many car drivers use natural gas as a fuel. *9* Ethanol does not produce harmful nitrous oxides or carbon monoxide, but its CO_2 emissions do contribute to global warming.

2 *1* Radon gas seeps into some houses and is a health risk. *2* It occurs naturally in the ground and is radioactive. *3* It enters houses through cracks in buildings, through cavity walls and around pipes. *4* Generally, the more uranium there is in the ground under the house, the more radon enters it. *5* When breathed in, it increases the risk of lung cancer. *6* Radiation leaks in nuclear power stations are another cause of cancer. *7* If the person who breathes in radon is also a smoker, the health risk is greatly increased. *8* There are various methods of preventing radon entering houses. *9* An obvious way is to block up cracks in the building. *10* The number of deaths attributed to radon each year is more than 2500.

● FIRST AND SECOND DRAFTS

1 Regard the first plan of an essay and your first draft as **provisional**.

2 As you write, your understanding of the topic grows. In the process, you sometimes feel you need to change your original plan. If so, do this:

- use your first draft to discover what **you** think.
- use your second draft to communicate this to your reader.
- be ready to rewrite at any stage. For example, suppose at first you accept one writer's description of the electric car as a 'pipe dream'. After all, pollution is caused in the production of electricity

for the car's batteries. As you write this down, this thought occurs to you: 'Is pollution caused in the generation of **all** electricity? What about solar power?' Perhaps you then read a little more to investigate the feasibility of generating electricity from the sun and decide that the electric car may be more of a possibility than you at first thought. If so, rewrite that section.

3 When looking critically at your first draft, consider these aspects (among others):

(a) the organization of your ideas
(b) the relevance of each point
(c) evidence to support your arguments: is it adequate?
(d) your tone and style: are they appropriate?
(e) your expression: would rephrasing improve any of your points?

● PROOF READING

This means checking your essay to make sure it is as well written and presented as you can make it and that there are no mistakes.

1 The key to this task is your mental approach to it.

2 Examine your piece of work as if it were written by someone else, and as if you have not seen it before. Be very critical.

3 People see what they expect to see. If you expect to see an essay without faults, that is what you will see. If you want to improve on your essay, look for trouble.

4 Do not just reread your essay superficially, in a relaxed, self-satisfied frame of mind, feeling good now that the job is done.

5 Read your work through twice.

6 On first reading, check the sense: look for
   – lack of clarity
   – ambiguities
   – contradictions
   – omitted evidence
   – omitted conclusions

Keep points like these in your mind as you read. Check your plan to confirm that you have left nothing out by mistake. Check that your points are in the best possible order.

7 On the second reading, examine the mechanical aspects of writing:
   – are your sentences grammatical?
   – is your spelling correct? Check proper names
   – is your punctuation correct?

Concentrate on these points all the time when proof reading.

PRACTICE

1 Choose an essay topic in connection with cars and the environment.

2 Read the notes on pages 108–110. Find other sources of information and make notes from them.

3 Plan an essay on this topic.   4 Write your first draft.

5 Study your first draft critically; consider any changes you should make to it.

6 Rewrite and proof read it.

While doing this work, bear in mind all the points covered in this chapter.

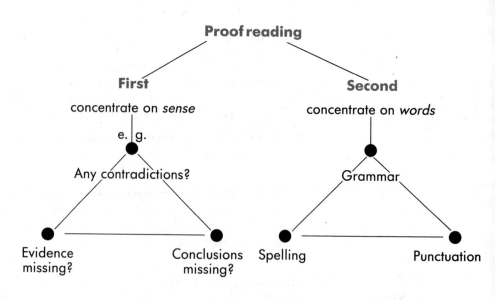

Proofreading

First — concentrate on *sense*
e.g. — Any contradictions?
— Evidence missing? — Conclusions missing?

Second — concentrate on *words*
— Grammar
— Spelling — Punctuation

NOTES

Notes A

(Source: 'What the Experts Say', G. Green, *The Car in the Future*, special *Times* supplement, 1990)

Expert 1: Lindsey Halstead, Chairman, Ford of Europe, ex-President, Ford of Brazil

'Partial' solutions to pollution by the motor car:

(a) **two-stroke** petrol engine: smaller engine, ∴ less fuel + emissions

(b) **electric vehicle**: problems:
    (i) high cost, low range, low performance
       ∴ not an alternative to petrol car
    (ii) charged from power stations
       ∴ only replacing one form of pollution with another
    (iii) battery technology would need to be improved

Notes B

(Source: 'The Answer to Car Pollution', *Blueprint for a Green Planet*, J. Seymour and H. Girardet, Dorling Kindersley)

Solutions

1 **Catalytic converter:**
Platinum catalyst forces harmful gases to inter-react, so very little toxic gas emitted. But (a) adds five per cent to cost of car
(b) adds five per cent to fuel consumption

2 **Lean-burn engine:**
Mixes more air with fuel: fewer exhaust gases.

3 **High-efficiency engine construction:**
Less friction, less fuel.

4 **Wider use of lead-free**

5 **Diesel:**
More economical with fuel but:
gives off carcinogenic soot particles –
diesel lorries very bad this way.

6 **'Localization':**
To reduce need for lorries, have many small-scale local factories instead of few big ones.

7 Other fuels:

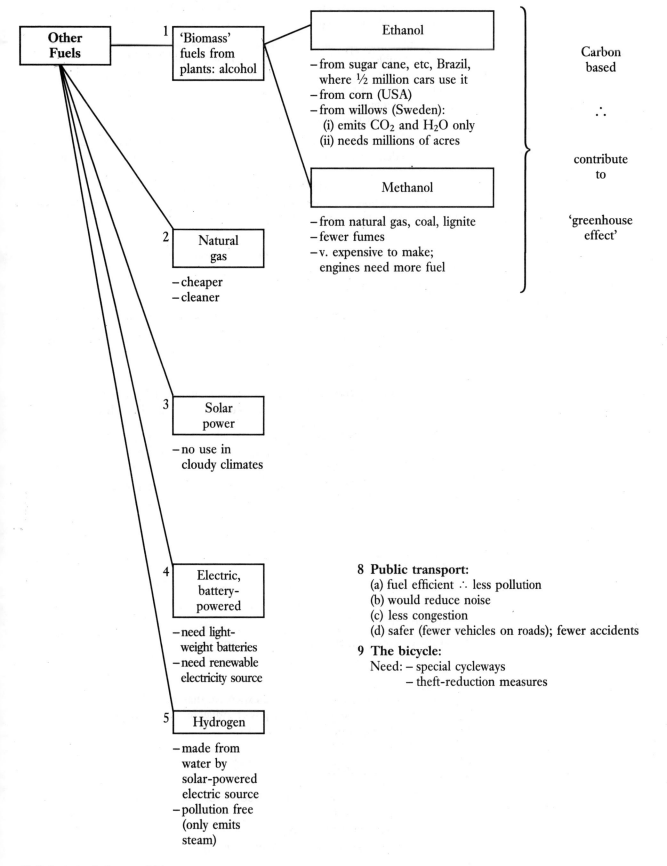

Other Fuels

1 'Biomass' fuels from plants: alcohol

Ethanol
– from sugar cane, etc, Brazil, where ½ million cars use it
– from corn (USA)
– from willows (Sweden):
  (i) emits CO_2 and H_2O only
  (ii) needs millions of acres

Methanol
– from natural gas, coal, lignite
– fewer fumes
– v. expensive to make; engines need more fuel

Carbon based

∴

contribute to

'greenhouse effect'

2 Natural gas
– cheaper
– cleaner

3 Solar power
– no use in cloudy climates

4 Electric, battery-powered
– need light-weight batteries
– need renewable electricity source

5 Hydrogen
– made from water by solar-powered electric source
– pollution free (only emits steam)

8 Public transport:
(a) fuel efficient ∴ less pollution
(b) would reduce noise
(c) less congestion
(d) safer (fewer vehicles on roads); fewer accidents

9 The bicycle:
Need: – special cycleways
– theft-reduction measures

Until alternative fuels are available, we should use fossil fuels more prudently.

Notes C

(Source: 'Powered by Hydrogen', R. Bell, *The Car in the Future*, *The Times* supplement, 1990)

1 A prototype BMW hydrogen-powered car is in use.

2 Hydrogen:
   (a) inexhaustible: two-thirds of earth's surface covered with H_2O
   (b) obtained by passing electric current through water. Could be done using electricity from the sun – no pollution
   (c) no pollutants
   (d) no CO_2 emissions (OK global warming)

3 **But** (a) H. is v. tricky to handle, only usable in **liquid** form: temp. $-253°$ C needed for this. Held in tank with 70 layers of aluminium foil and glassfibre for insulation
   (b) refuelling: takes skilled technicians one hour to refill tank
   (c) production of H. very expensive, also storage and distribution
   (d) even when compressed, large amounts are needed: 20.5 gallons for 150 miles

4 Consortium of German companies building a pilot hydrogen-producing plant – based on solar energy.

5 BMW is looking 100 years ahead. Or 50? Or 30? No one knows.

Notes D

(Source: 'Electric Cars on Trial', S. Baker, *Observer Magazine*, April 15, 1990)

	1 Peugeot's Vert:	2 GM's Impact
Range:	75 miles	124 miles
Top speed:	62 mph	100mph
Acceleration:	more than twice standard time	0–60 in eight secs (standard)
Recharging time:	10 hours	two hours

Notes E

(Source: 'Watt Car', B. Fraser and G. Kacher, *The Car in the Future*, *The Times* supplement, 1990)

To make GM's *Impact* viable must:

1 Halve cost of electric motors.

2 Greatly lengthen battery life. Battery life now around 32 000 km. GM's engineers reckon to extend to 70 000 km in a couple of years.

3 Make batteries lighter and more compact.

4 Reduce cost: electricity charge more expensive than equivalent petrol. But 'if California would make cheap solar power available, Impact owners could save money'.

ANSWERS

Practice 1 on page 105
1 Wrong proportions: more space needed for improved public transport.
2 Suitable proportions.
3 Not enough on hydrogen cars.
4 Too much space given to battery technology.

Practice on page 106
Sentences **not** contributing to the central idea:
Question **1**: *3, 4, 8.*   Question **2**: *6, 8, 9.*

Chapter 13
Projects and coursework

THE PURPOSE OF THIS CHAPTER

A project means all the work associated with investigating a question or designing and making an object and then writing an account of the process. This chapter examines and identifies the main aspects that are essential for compiling and writing project work. In order to do this effectively, it is broken down into these sections:

- You and your project work
- Skills
- Title
- Diary
- Method of enquiry
- Collection of data
- Asking questions: questionnaires
- Presenting data
- Analysis of results
- Conclusion
- Organizing your report

● YOU AND YOUR PROJECT WORK

A project can be a great opportunity for you to pursue a topic that interests you personally. The particular question that you, or you and a partner, investigate will be unique to you, so you will have considerable freedom to decide for yourself how to conduct your enquiry. You can become deeply involved in it, show your understanding of the subject and demonstrate your energy and skills. A project is a worthwhile and enjoyable challenge resulting in a major piece of work that you will be proud to show to others.

Your teacher will be your main source of guidance and will help you in the choice of title and your method of enquiry. But use other people as sources, too, particularly staff in museums and public libraries and any adults you know who can help you because of the work they do.

● SKILLS

A crucial purpose in carrying out a project is to show that you have certain skills. So if your title is, for example, 'Does Shaftesbury need an additional car park?', it is not necessary for you to provide overwhelming proof one way or the other. But you must show that you:

- have chosen an appropriate method of enquiry into this question.
- can plan and organize your enquiry.
- have observed and recorded data accurately.
- can present results in the form of tables, diagrams, graphs, and so on.
- are able to analyze the results.
- can draw an appropriate conclusion.

Certain subjects require and often demand the use of specific skills when researching and compiling projects. The Southern Examining

Group *Teachers' Guide* lists the following essentials to be shown in history projects:

(a) evaluation and interpretation of sources
(b) selection of relevant material
(c) empathetic reconstruction of the ways of thinking and feeling of a people of a different time or place
(d) analysis of causation and motivation
(e) analysis of the role of the individual in history

For CDT projects, the following skills should be shown:

- graphic communication and a production drawing
- skills of workmanship in making an artefact

As you work on a project, reflect from time to time on the skills that are expected. Make sure that you are demonstrating them at each point of your enquiry. For GCSE, show that you 'know, understand and can do'.

PRACTICE

Find out what skills you are expected to show for a project in one of your subjects. Make a list of them.

● **TITLE**

Making a good choice of title is crucial to the success of a project. Bear these points in mind:

1 In most cases a project should be an investigation into a question, the testing of a hypothesis or, in CDT, the identifying of a need and the attempt to satisfy it. It is not just a description. You would not, for example, describe the existing shoe shops in a town, but you might answer the question 'Is there a demand for another shoe shop in the town?'.

2 The title should be specific and not too broad. Not 'Does public transport in Leeds need to be improved?' but 'Would an improved city bus service reduce traffic congestion in the centre of Leeds?'.

3 Before you decide on a title and start working on your actual investigation, you must be able to see how you will conduct every stage of your enquiry. You must be reasonably sure that it will 'work out'. This means making a trial plan – a plan to test if the idea is feasible. One of the main frustrations felt when doing a project is the gradual realization that 'it isn't going to work out'. You feel you will have to start again with another title and a totally different enquiry and that you have wasted time by pursuing a line that led nowhere. To avoid this situation, make a plan of how you will conduct the enquiry. List all the steps in your project, even down to the questions you may ask in a questionnaire and how you will analyze the data yielded by your investigations. Only decide on your title when you are reasonably certain that you will be able to see the project through to completion. Remember that you can ask for your teacher's guidance in doing this.

4 It is necessary to be realistic. Ask yourself 'Is this an enquiry that I am able to carry out?'. Will it, for example, require travel that you cannot undertake? Will it deal with sensitive matters which your informants may not wish to discuss? Does it involve speaking to people who may be too busy to spare you the time? Is it too dangerous? If it is a CDT project, does it require costly materials that you can't obtain? Discuss these questions with your teacher.

5 The project must enable you to demonstrate the skills which are expected. Assess the title you are considering in the light of this need.

● DIARY

From the beginning keep a diary to record what you do and your reflections on how your project is developing. This enables you to:

- retain important facts and ideas for your report.
- write up the section of the report where you describe the method of your enquiry. You will be assessed on this.

For example, suppose you found while interviewing people that a particular question led to answers which you could not analyze. If you decided to change the question as a result, you would need to describe this process and explain it in your report. You would draw on notes that you had made in your diary.

● METHOD OF ENQUIRY

In your title you ask a question or put forward a hypothesis for testing. It is necessary to satisfy yourself that your method of enquiry will indeed answer the question or put the hypothesis to a real test. At an early stage think out the details of the methods you will use. Suppose, for example, your title is 'Does Shaftesbury need an additional car park?'. What data will answer this question? Will it be enough on one Saturday morning to ask motorists who have just parked their cars how long it took them to find a parking place? Or is it better to ask: 'Did it take you longer than it should have done?' How reliable will their answers be? How many will you need to ask? What about other days of the week? What about different times of the day? And if you find mid-morning and mid-afternoon on weekdays motorists spent an average of seven and a half minutes looking for a place to park, what can you conclude from that? Should you combine the results of a questionnaire with, say, your observations of the extent of illegal parking at certain times? Will you also examine local plans for new housing estates around the town, by-pass plans, plans for new shop developments, plans for improving public transport, trends in car-ownership, etc?

Before you embark on the collection of such data, make sure it will enable you to reach a conclusion of some useful kind for your project.

● COLLECTION OF DATA

Data is of two kinds: primary and secondary. Primary data is what you obtain by observation, measurement and asking questions. Secondary data is what you obtain from printed or recorded sources or what other people have collected. In some subjects, for example, geography, most of your data will be primary. In others it will be mainly secondary.

1 Collect only the data you need.

2 If your data is a drawing, a sketch, the taking of a photograph, making a measurement, or something similar, do make a note of **what** the sketch or photograph (etc) is of, **where** it was, **when** you made it and so on. Note all relevant details because if you include diagrams, sketches, etc, in your project, they must be properly labelled.

3 If your data is secondary, do record the source of it. If it is a publication, note:

 – its title
 – its author
 – its publisher
 – the date of the edition you are using
 – the page(s) on which your data appears

It is vital to include this information about any secondary source you quote. If you do not acknowledge sources, examiners will take the view that you are trying to pass off information as your own when it is not.

4 Keep notes of all relevant aspects of your collecting process. If, for example, certain types of people, or large numbers, do not accept your questionnaire, record this: it may be important in discussing your results.

5 Be accurate in any measurements you make.

6 Be safe in anything you undertake. Do not stand in a dangerous place to observe traffic and be careful near rivers and steep slopes.

● ASKING QUESTIONS

A questionnaire is the list of questions you use when conducting a survey. You can either distribute it to people to fill in at their leisure or use it to conduct an interview, completing one questionnaire per person. When designing a questionnaire:

- give it a short title; include your name and the date.
- do not have too short or too long a list of questions.
- present your questions in a logical order.
- set out your questions neatly on the page.
- keep the questions short and simple, each dealing with only one item of information.
- each question should be clear and unambiguous.
- avoid questions that express an opinion, like 'Do you buy environmentally-harmful products?'

Kinds of questions

They are of two types:
1 Closed: the answer is limited to choices given on the questionnaire, .

e.g. **Sex** Male ☐ Female ☐

2 Open-ended: the person answering is not restricted,
e.g. **What is your favourite vegetable?** ....

The answers to closed questions are easy to analyse, but they can lead to oversimplification of a situation. Open-ended answers may be hard to group together for analysis, but they are likely to give accurate information.

PRACTICE

1 Which questions on the specimen questionnaire that follows are closed and which open-ended?

2 Do you have any criticisms of any of these questions in the light of the points made above?

114

Specimen questionnaire

Survey of student purchases from Semley shop

Interviewer: J. James **Date:** ....

1 Sex
Male ☐   **2 Age**   11 ☐ 12 ☐ 13 ☐ 14 ☐
Female ☐   15 ☐ 16 ☐ 17 ☐ 18 ☐

3 Indicate what you bought *most recently* from Semley shop:

choc bar ☐   other sweet ☐   soft drink ☐

savoury snack ☐ magazine ☐   cosmetics ☐

stationery ☐   other (please say what) ....

4 On what date did you buy it? ....

5 What item is your *most common* purchase from this shop?

choc bar ☐   other sweet ☐   soft drink ☐

savoury snack ☐ magazine ☐   cosmetics ☐

stationery ☐   other (please say what) ....

6 What item (at present not in the shop) would you *most like* the shop to sell? ....

Thank you for your help.

Sampling

Questionnaires are given to a sample of people to find out information about a whole 'population'. The population in question may be 'people who visit Doncaster', 'pupils in St. Andrew's school', etc. It is important that those to whom you give a questionnaire should be representative, i.e. typical, of the 'population'. You would not get useful information, for example, if you only gave it to female shoppers when you were investigating shoppers of both sexes. In short, your sampling must be random.

1 You may achieve a random distribution by taking, for example, every sixth motorist at a car park or every tenth name from a list.

2 You may achieve it by taking names out of a hat, rather than by giving questionnaires to your friends, say.

3 You may adopt a quota method, e.g. by asking two students (randomly selected) from each class or by interviewing an equal number from each age group, e.g. 10 aged 10–20, 10 aged 21–30, 10 aged 31–40, etc.

4 Your sample must be large enough to give a result that is more than just a matter of opinion or speculation. Thirty is probably the minimum. You would discuss sample size, reasons for it and the effect on your results when writing up your project.

Safety

Be safety conscious when you go out interviewing.

1 Your school should give instructions which must be followed to the letter.

2 Carry your teacher's letter of authority.

3 Tell someone where you are going and when you will return.

4 Interview in daylight, not in the dark.

5 Choose safe, not lonely or dangerous places.

6 Interview with another person if possible.

7 Take with you coins or a card for a public telephone.

Courtesy

Be courteous when interviewing:

- if you know in advance that you wish to interview a particular person, arrange a time to suit their convenience.
- approach people with a smile.
- briefly explain your purpose and ask if they will be kind enough to help.
- if a person is unwilling, do not try to make them help you.
- explain that the information will be confidential.
- remember to thank people.

PRACTICE

Design a questionnaire for a survey of your own choice. Here are some suggestions:

1 You want to compare the eating habits of different age groups.

2 You want to investigate people's leisure activities in connection with existing or proposed leisure centres.

3 You want to answer a question you have about some aspect of public or private transport in your area.

● PRESENTING DATA

After the collection of data, this is the next step in handling it. It is necessary for you to include in your written project the data that will make a contribution to it. You will be given marks for showing various presentation skills. So find out what skills of this kind are required for your subject. You are likely to have to show that you can:

- use a variety of techniques (not just graphs and pie charts).
- select **relevant** data and present it in an **appropriate** form.
- transfer information from field notes, surveys, etc, **accurately**.
- label and number diagrams, sketches, etc.
- refer in your text to your diagrams, sketches, tables, etc.

It may be appropriate to use a computer to process some of your data. If this would help your project, you ought to do it and present the results in a suitable way.

You are not likely to present all your data at one point in your report. Each presentation should be placed near the section of your text that refers to it.

1 Tables It is often right to present data in its simplest form first, i.e. in the form of a table, and to follow this with other techniques.

2 Graphs You may well use a graph to show a trend: a development of something over a period of time, e.g. 'the number of hours of daily exercise for different age groups'. See also the chapter on science skills, page 156.

3 Pie charts These show how large each section of a whole is, compared with the other sections. For example, if all the students in a school are aged between 13 and 19, a pie chart could show what proportion are of each age.

4 Bar graphs These are often used to compare the data for two similar groups, e.g. to compare the numbers of private cars and commercial vehicles passing a particular point at different times of the day, as shown below.

Bar graphs are suitable when one piece of information, e.g. that 26 commercial vehicles passed a certain point between 7.00 and 7.30 a.m., is separate from other pieces of information. Data on a bar graph does not indicate a trend: for continuous data, use a line graph.

5 Histograms Histograms give a good visual comparison of a set of similar groups, e.g. to compare how full four city car parks were at 10 a.m. on a Saturday morning. The histogram shown overleaf shows a development of this technique: it compares the same car parks at two different times.

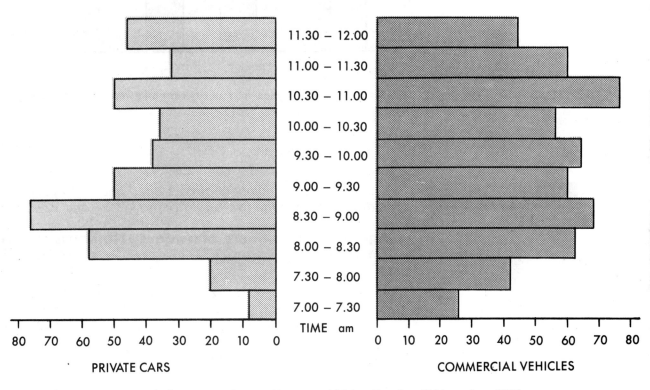

Vehicles passing Grange House on A304 on Tuesday 13 November, 1990

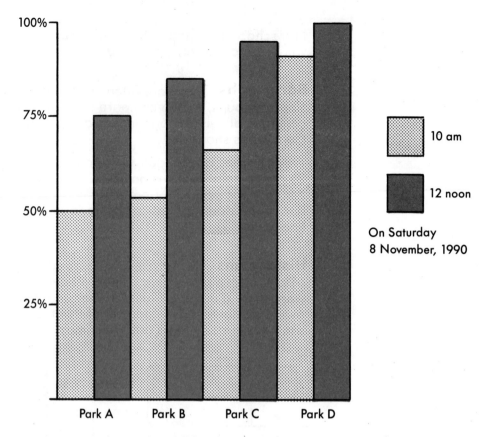

Histogram showing how full four city car parks were at 10 am and 12 noon.

This table shows the numbers of cars aged one to 10 years old owned by people in the two age groups: 17–21 and 22–26.

Age of car in years	Numbers of owners aged 17–21	Numbers of owners aged 22–26
10	6	3
9	6	4
8	10	6
7	16	10
6	15	13
5	20	16
4	14	22
3	7	12
2	4	9
1	2	5

Draw a histogram comparing the numbers of people in each age group who owned cars of each age.

In addition to the above techniques, use sketches, maps, diagrams and photographs where appropriate. Try to think of interesting and imaginative ways of presenting data. Use pictograms, scatter graphs, chloropleths, examples of these are shown opposite. If you are comparing two sets of data, do make sure that the methods you use bring out the comparison effectively.

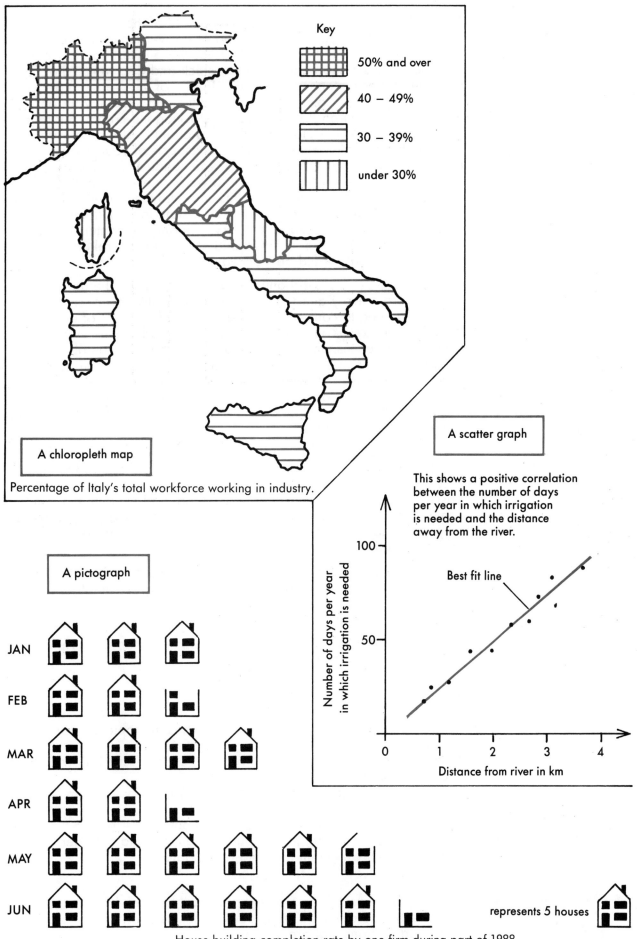

Key

50% and over

40 – 49%

30 – 39%

under 30%

A chloropleth map

Percentage of Italy's total workforce working in industry.

A scatter graph

This shows a positive correlation between the number of days per year in which irrigation is needed and the distance away from the river.

Best fit line

100

Number of days per year in which irrigation is needed

50

0   1   2   3   4

Distance from river in km

A pictograph

JAN

FEB

MAR

APR

MAY

JUN

represents 5 houses

House building completion rate by one firm during part of 1988.

● ANALYSIS OF RESULTS

This is the discussion of your data in the light of the question your project has asked. Consider what sort of answer the data provides. How convincing is it? For example, if you were investigating what additional lines a shop could usefully stock and discovered that 75 per cent of those interviewed were in favour of ice-cream, 8 per cent fast foods and 5 per cent novels, then you could state in your analysis that there was a strong preference for stocking ice-cream. But before you came to the conclusion that the shop ought to stock ice-cream, you should also take into account other aspects of your enquiry, especially the circumstances in which you conducted it. For example, if your survey was conducted during a week of exceptionally hot weather, you should mention that this could have influenced the views of those you asked. You might, therefore, state in your analysis that it would be necessary to repeat the survey during the winter and then compare the results of both surveys to obtain a more reliable indication of what should be stocked.

If you have used a questionnaire, you must discuss the data obtained from every question. For example, in the corner shop survey you would need to consider the preferences of students of each age and of both sexes. You would want to weigh up both the measure of student preferences, namely the results from the question about the most recent purchase and the one about the most common purchase. What do the answers tell you? If you find that there is a strong preference for choc bars among 11–13 year olds, this may have a bearing on the type of choc bars the shop should stock: those with an appeal for this age group.

The writing skills you will use will be partly those of argument (see page 99). Remember to consider evidence 'on the other side', that is, data which conflicts with the interpretation you are reaching on the basis of most of the data. Try to understand, and explain, how you come to have conflicting data. If you suspect there was a flaw in the way you conducted the enquiry, discuss it. State any reservations about the validity of your data.

Do not pad out your report with irrelevant points. Remember that quality is what is needed and this is not the same as length.

If you worked on the project with a partner, do indicate, as precisely as you can, the contribution made by each of you. For example, state who took each photograph, how many interviews each conducted, and so on.

● CONCLUSION

In your conclusion:

- refer to the question or hypothesis which is the topic of your project.
- state the conclusions you have reached on this issue following your analysis of the data.
- summarize any important aspects of your enquiry, e.g. any special problems.
- mention any interesting matters arising out of it.
- look to the future, suggest a course of action, and consider possible future work in the area investigated.

● ORGANIZING YOUR REPORT

The outline suggested on the next page will be useful for many projects. But do discuss it with your teacher as your topic or subject may need sections that are different from those given here.

Title page
Table of contents
Introduction: the queston to be investigated
Main body: the method of your investigation,
   results and your analysis of them
Conclusion
Appendix: if needed
List of sources

An appendix is used for data which is too extensive to include in the main body of your report. The list of sources will be in alphabetical order of authors' surnames, giving title, date of publication and publisher.

ANSWERS

Practice on page 114

1 Closed questions: 1, 2.
  Open-ended questions: 4, 6.
  Questions 3 and 5 are mixed. If a box is ticked, the answer is 'closed'; if the interviewee writes his or her own answer after the word 'other', it is 'open'.
2 It is for you to say!

Practice on page 118

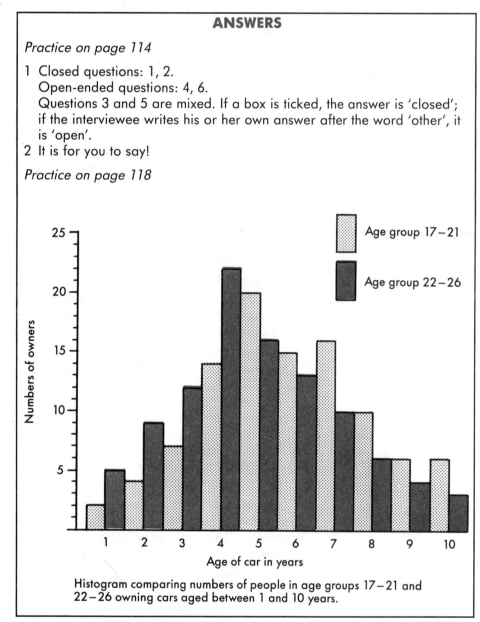

Histogram comparing numbers of people in age groups 17–21 and 22–26 owning cars aged between 1 and 10 years.

Chapter 14
Revision techniques

THE PURPOSE OF THIS CHAPTER

This chapter aims to provide you with a variety of techniques for revising. It covers the following topics:

- Making a revision timetable
- Revising at intervals
- Active revision
- Revision slips
- Reducing notes to essential points
- Flexibility
- Enjoyment

● MAKING A REVISION TIMETABLE

The golden rule of revision is to allow enough time for it! You will probably need about three months and this will include both holiday and term time.

1 Hours available
Work out the total number of hours you can use for revision during weekdays and weekends in the holidays, and during weekdays and weekends in term time.

2 Holiday time
Make use of as much holiday time as possible since there will be more pressure on your time during the term because of other school activities and responsibilities.

3 Last fortnight
Leave the last fortnight before the exams out of your calculations for the moment, for these reasons:
(a) it is an opportunity for a last, short revision of the most essential points or of those needing more attention
(b) it is a chance to catch up if you have missed revision through ill health or for any other reason
(c) It allows you a few days of reduced pressure before the exams so that you can approach them fresh and interested

4 More/less time
Take into account which subjects will need more revision time and which less. This may be related to your personal strengths and weaknesses or to the nature of the subject.

5 Make timetable
You are now ready to map your subjects on to particular hours on your revision timetable.

PRACTICE

Working backwards from the date of your first exam, calculate all the time you will have available for revision over a period of three months. Present this as a timetable but without yet writing in your specific subjects.

Making a revision timetable

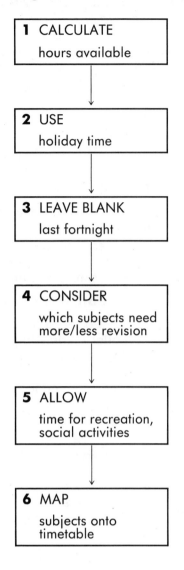

1 CALCULATE
hours available

↓

2 USE
holiday time

↓

3 LEAVE BLANK
last fortnight

↓

4 CONSIDER
which subjects need
more/less revision

↓

5 ALLOW
time for recreation,
social activities

↓

6 MAP
subjects onto
timetable

● **REVISING AT INTERVALS**

To retain information in your mind, it is not usually enough to revise it only once. You need to revise any given topic several times, at ever-increasing intervals. Four revision sessions per individual topic, e.g. magnetism, or the causes of the English Civil War, over the three month period would be ideal. However, you may not have time to fit in as many as four revisions of each topic. If so, try for three, with the second one only a few days after the first.

When it comes to mapping your subjects on to particular hours on your timetable, you can either:

(a) revise **all** your biology, then **all** all your history, then **all** your French, and so on

or (b) revise **some** biology, then **some** history, then **some** French, and when you have revised some of each subject, revise **more** biology, then **more** history, **more** French and so on

The advantage of method (b) is that you do not get fed up by spending a long time on just one subject, and by keeping up the interest in this way you will probably retain information more easily.

Whatever you ultimately decide to do about timetabling your revision **You must**:

● have a plan of some kind.
● start early enough.
● keep up with your revision programme and stick to it!

● ACTIVE REVISION

Do not simply read your notes over and over again. If you do this:

● you are using little or no brain power.
● it is boring.
● it doesn't fix things in your mind effectively.
● after doing it, you have no idea whether or not you have committed the essentials of the topic to your memory.

Instead, revise **actively**, that is, **do** something as you revise.

1 Have a large quantity of pieces of scrap paper to hand. It doesn't matter if something is already written on the back of them.
2 Have a pen or pencil in your hand.
3 Study a section of your notes.
4 Try to commit to memory the essential points.
5 Then put your notes out of sight.
6 From your memory write down the essential points on a piece of the scrap paper.
7 Look again at your notes. Check that the points you made on the scrap paper are **correct** and **complete**.
8 Note any points that are **wrong** or **omitted**. Then concentrate on committing these to memory.

The flow chart below shows a summary of this procedure.

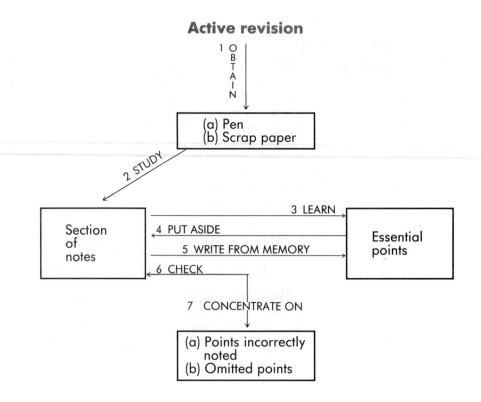

Active revision

clear theme to them. This also allows important linking of ideas. Thus question 2 made reference to farming, population, industry and urbanization and question 5 referred to energy and industry.

This was one of the questions referred to:

2 With reference to one or more Economically Less Developed Countries explain how changes in agriculture and village life are linked to:
(i) the growth in towns;
(ii) the growth in industry.

● ENJOYMENT

Try to make your revision a pleasant experience. If you enjoy it, you will do more revision than if you dislike it. So it is important—and pleasant—to make it fun. Here are some ideas:

1 Avoid revision sessions that are too long. Work for a medium length of time, then have a short break. Then revise again and break off briefly again.

2 Do use the active method of revision—with a pen and paper. It is much more satisfying than any passive form of revision.

3 From time to time revise with others. But make sure that this time is spent on genuine revision work and is not wasted in social chatting.

4 If time permits, investigate a detail that interests you by doing a little new reading on the subject. This can be very refreshing and, of course, adds to your knowledge bank.

5 At the end of the day, list the topics you have revised. From this you will gain a sense of achievement!

ANSWERS

Practice on page 126

1 (a) Essential points: Young, Older men, Unskilled workers, Married with many children, Ethnic minorities.
(b) Mnemonic of initial letters: YOU and ME.

The advantages of active revision are:

1 You are doing something active with your brain and hands. This prevents boredom and keeps up interest in your work.

2 You will know exactly which points you are able to remember and which you can't. You then know that you must make a special effort to learn the points you got wrong or left out.

3 You will gain a sense of achievement and progress every time you get a positive result from using this method.

● REVISION SLIPS

Make use of otherwise wasted time for revision. We all have time when we are doing nothing, for example, when travelling in a car, bus or train; when waiting for someone; when waiting in a queue, for the dentist, doctor, hairdresser; or even when waiting for a lesson to begin!

Characteristics of living things

All living things show certain characteristics which distinguish them from non-living things:
R for Respiration: release of energy from food.
E for Excretion: removal of waste products of metabolism (chemical reactions within cells).
M for Movement: parts or whole of the body.
I for Irritability: sensing changes in the surroundings and responding to them.
N for Nutrition: making or eating food.
De for Development and growth: increase in size and complexity.
R for Reproduction: making of new organisms similar to the parent or parents.

Memory aid: REMINDeR

(Adapted from *Keyfacts Passcards GCSE Biology*, J. Hassall, Charles Letts & Co Ltd)

1 Make small rectangles of paper, each about a quarter the size of this page, or buy some index cards.

2 Use one such piece of paper or index card for a particular topic that you have chosen.

3 Write on it, neatly (i) the name of the topic, e.g. 'Characteristics of living things' and (ii) the main points to remember on this topic.

4 You will make several of these revision slips on various topics during one week.

5 Clip them together and keep them with you.

6 Revise them (**actively**) whenever you have a spare moment. Do this by yourself or with a friend.

7 Write 'Week 1' on another slip of paper and clip it to the front of your slips that you have made and revised in the first week. Then make, revise and collect slips for 'Week 2', 'Week 3', and so on.

An example of one of these slips is shown on page 125.

PRACTICE

1 *Make revision slips for any three topics chosen from your subjects.*

2 *List five occasions in the next few days when you will have the opportunity to revise them.*

● REDUCING NOTES TO ESSENTIAL POINTS

You should find this process a useful revision aid. Looking back to the example of the revision slip you should be able to see that the characteristics of living things have been reduced to seven words:

Respiration
Excretion
Movement
Irritability
Nutrition
Development
Reproduction

Each word should be sufficient to act as a 'trigger' to enable you to explain its fuller meaning as given in your notes. However, it is possible to go even further and devise a mnemonic: the initial letters of the seven words make the word REMINDeR. Remember that, and you should be able to give a good account of the characteristics of living things!

PRACTICE

1 *Unemployment is a topic that is studied in economics. Here is a set of notes on one aspect of it.*

(a) Reduce this list to a handful of essential points.

(b) Invent a suitable mnemonic for them.

People most affected by unemployment

1 Young: people aged 16–25 because:
 – it is expensive to train and pay them
 – they have less skill and experience
 – of the 'last in, first out' principle
 – employers don't have to pay them so much in redundancy money

2 Older men: because of their declining productivity.

3 Unskilled workers: because they are the most likely employees to be replaced by new technology.

4 Married people: if they have lots of children: a father of four children is much more likely to be unemployed than a father of one: because of state benefits the incentive to work is reduced.

5 Ethnic minorities: a male West Indian school leaver with good public examination results is twice as likely to be unemployed as his white counterpart.

2 *Reduce a set of your own notes to a few key words and make up a mnemonic for them.*

3 *Choose one of the sets of notes on the car and the environment (p.108–110) and reduce them to key words and devise a mnemonic.*

● FLEXIBILITY

It is important to know the content of your notes. But you should not expect that all your exam questions will be so phrased or set out as to allow you simply to reproduce the points in your notes in the form in which you have recorded them.

Examiners often design questions in a way that requires you to select points from different aspects of a topic, or from different topics and different sets of notes and then combine these selected points in your answer. So:

● be flexible in your attitude to your notes.
● look through recent exam papers and find questions that require you to pick out only certain points from a set of notes or to rearrange the ideas in some way.
● make outline plans for such essays.
● think out what information that you already know is applicable to a particular question. You may have more relevant information than you realize at first.
● avoid becoming so mentally fixed on your notes that you can only draw on them in the pattern in which you having been learning them.

To underline this point, here is an extract from the Northern Examining Association's report on the 1989 GCSE geography examination paper:

Candidates coped well with the way that this paper often mixed up topics within question. This technique was used to try to ensure that there was a fuller syllabu coverage than in the past whilst still allowing the use of extended questions with

Chapter 15
Final preparation and the exam

THE PURPOSE OF THIS CHAPTER

This chapter shows you how best to prepare yourself in the run-up to your examinations and what to do when you finally get into the examination room! It is in two parts:
Part 1: Preparation for the examination.
Part 2: The examination itself.

Part 1 deals with the following points:
- Analyzing and answering questions
- Question formats (multiple choice, structured, part-page/whole-page answers, essays)
- Practical exams
- Becoming familiar with syllabuses and exam papers
- Your mental and physical fitness for the exam
- Dividing your time between exam questions

Part 2 deals with these points:
- What to do when you have the exam paper before you
- Answering short answer questions
- Answering essay questions
- What do to at the end of the examination

Remember that the better prepared you are for a task, the easier it will be and the more confident you will feel about it.

PART 1 PREPARATION FOR THE EXAMINATION

● **ANALYZING AND ANSWERING QUESTIONS**

Examiners, in their reports, stress that the single factor that wins or loses most marks for candidates is the **relevance** of their answers. So practise doing the following:

(a) **analyze** exam questions very carefully
(b) **work out** exactly what the questions require you to do, and do that
(c) **avoid** writing all you know on a topic merely because you see a familiar expression like 'Thirty Years War' or 'chlorophyll'.

The following quotations from examiners' reports shows the importance of relevance:

1 A worrying number of candidates totally misread the question and thus misdirected the answer.
2 Too much irrelevance. This was particularly evident in questions about . . .
3 The most persistent weakness was a failure to answer the question actually asked; too many candidates preferred to answer the question they would like to have been asked, or even just put down on paper all they knew on a topic. Teachers are strongly urged to practise their students in the art of analyzing carefully the precise meaning of examination questions and preparing detailed plans for answers.
4 In (b) (ii) an **explanation** (stressed) was required for the results. Most candidates gave a purely descriptive account of the results as shown by the graph. Candidates should learn to distinguish the difference between description and explanation.

5 The most common weakness was to simply paraphrase or quote at length, rather than to explain or discuss the extracts

(Extracts 1, 2, 3 and 5 from the Report on the June 1988 A level examinations, History and Archaeology; extract 4 from the Report on the June 1988 A level Biological Sciences examinations; Cambridge University Local Examinations Syndicate)

Examiners also stress the need to distinguish between (a) narrating, i.e. saying **what** happened and (b) explaining, i.e. saying **why** it happened.

Detailed example of a question and the examiners' comments

2A (i) Describe how the way of life of the Plains Indians fitted in with their environment.

Examiner's comment: Too many candidates concentrated on the life-style of the Plains Indians, failing to relate this to their environment.

● If the question asks you to relate one thing to another, it is essential to do so.

2A (iii) Explain why the way of life of the Plains Indians had changed by the end of the nineteenth century.

Examiner's comment: The question clearly asked candidates to explain **why** the way of life of the Plains Indians had changed: many candidates simply described the changes.

● If you are asked to explain **why**, it is vital to do so.

(Both questions taken from NEA GCSE History, June 1989)

PRACTICE

1 *This question is from the NEA GCSE English literature paper taken in June 1989:*

Write about other examples of revenge in the novel as a whole that: **are** sweet
    are **not** sweet.
What is the minimum number of examples that you must mention in order to answer this question?

2 *Find past questions in your own subjects and make detailed plans after analyzing what each requires.*

● QUESTION FORMATS

Be prepared for the different question formats that you will encounter in the exam and make sure you are familiar with each.

Multiple choice questions

These are questions where you select the right answer from two or more choices that you are given. Questions of this kind take several forms. For example:

1 Which food supplies the most energy?
  A 1g fibre.
  B 1g carbohydrate.
  C 1g protein.
  D 1g fat.
(From NEA GCSE Science, June 1989)

2 Match the names from the following list of substances with the correct formula in the table below.

hydrogen, nitrogen oxide, sulphur trioxide, water

Formula	Name
(i) H_2	
(ii) SO_3	
(iii) H_2O	
(iv) NO_2	

(From WJEC GCSE Science, June 1989)

3 Study the diagram below, a graph which shows the relationship between energy consumption and gross national product (GNP) per person.

1 Burkina Faso
2 India
3 Tanzania
4 Kenya
5 Indonesia
6 Egypt
7 Zambia
8 Peru
9 Mexico
10 Brazil
11 Uruguay
12 Argentina
13 Venezuela
14 USSR
15 Italy
16 United Kingdom
17 Japan
18 Saudi Arabia
19 Australia
20 West Germany
21 USA

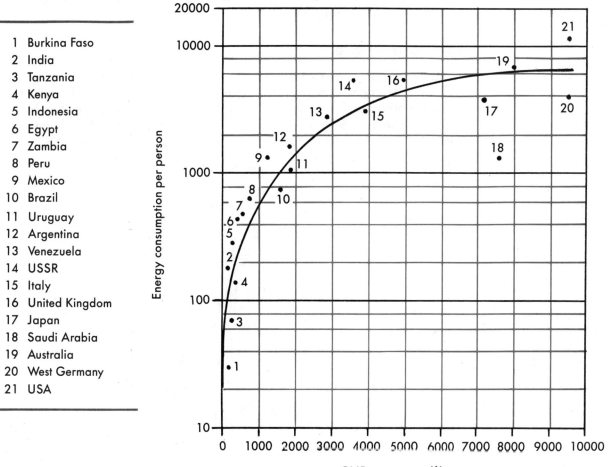

Complete the following statements by crossing out the incorrect words.

A
The best fit line shows that, in general, the more energy a country uses the $\frac{higher}{lower}$ is the GNP.

B
The steep part of the best-fit line represents the $\frac{\textbf{Developing}}{\textbf{Developed}}$ World, while the section with the gentler slope represents the $\frac{\textbf{Developing}}{\textbf{Developed}}$ World.

(From LEAG GCSE Geography, June 1989)

Bear these points in mind:

1 Read *all* the choices and understand a question thoroughly before answering it.

2 If one question is proving difficult, don't stay too long on it. Go on to the next one and remember to return to the difficult one later.

3 If you cannot decide between two of the options and time is running out, make the best estimate you can of the right answer.

4 Don't leave any question unanswered: there is no penalty for a wrong answer.

5 When checking, consider mainly whether you have marked a wrong option through carelessness and whether you have understood questions. Do not be quick to change answers you have already thought carefully about: there is a danger of changing a correct answer to a wrong one.

Structured questions

These are questions that consist of several parts, all related to one topic. Clear instructions are given for each part and the number of marks that can be obtained for each part is usually stated. Questions of this kind often present data for comprehension or interpretation. Here is an example from the MEG GCSE biology paper taken in June 1989:

1 The diagram shows the human alimentary canal and associated organs.

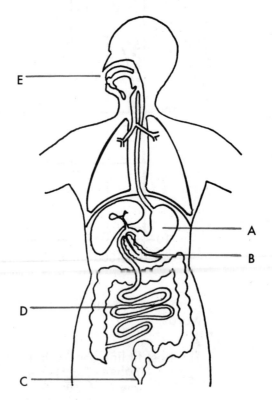

(a) (i) The diagram is labelled **A** to **E**. Using these letters only, answer questions 1, 2 and 3.

1 The position where food is ingested is labelled _____

2 Fat digestion takes place at _____

3 Food is egested from _____ (3)

(ii) Name the process which moves food from **D** to **C**.

_____ (1)

(iii) State **two** functions of **B**.

1 _____

2 _____ (2)

(b) (i) Name **one** factor which affects the way a digestive enzyme works.

_____ (1)

(ii) If you were investigating the effect of the factor named in (b)(i), name **another** factor you would have to control.

_____ (1)

(iii) How would you do this? _____

_____

_____

_____ (2)

With questions of this type it is particularly important to read the question carefully and do precisely what you are asked to do. In the above question, for example, you must know what is meant by the words **process**, **function** and **factor** and state exactly those pieces of information. When asked 'How would you do this?', you must state the **methods** you would use, the **steps** you would take.

Learn, by practising with a time limit, to divide your time wisely between the parts of such questions. The above example is one of six questions for which there is a total of 40 minutes, with 10 marks per question. That includes the time needed to read and understand the questions.

Part-page/whole-page answers

Some questions give you a number of lines or a whole page of lines to write down an answer or part of one. For example:

Write an explanatory account of the origins of mid-oceanic ridges in terms of plate tectonic theory.   (*5 marks*)

(From WJEC A level Geography, June 1989)

Seven lines are made available. For questions like this:

1 Get used to calculating fast the amount of time you should assign to your answer.

2 To do this, always take into account the marks available. In the exam from which the question above was taken, for example, candidates were required to answer six questions in three hours, i.e. **under** 30 minutes each (allowing for time to read and select questions). Each question is worth 20 marks. So five marks represents one quarter of the marks for one question. So how long should you spend on the origins of mid-oceanic ridges, i.e. how long is a quarter of just under 30 minutes?

3 Write concisely (see 'Writing skills 1' on page 98). For the example question above you would write one paragraph. Go straight to your first point.

4 Use appropriate language. In the geography question on mid-oceanic ridges you are dealing with **causes** (origins). Turn to page 145 to find some useful expressions.

The rubrics for this geography exam allow you extra lines at the back of the answer book **if you make extensive deletions to your answers**. They warn you, if you use this extra space, to identify carefully the question parts you are reanswering. Heed advice like this.

If you have a whole page, quickly decide how to divide up your topic, e.g. into two or three paragraphs. This forces you to make a mental plan and organize your information.

Essay-type questions

Chapters 11 and 12 provided guidance on writing skills. For an essay question you should apply these skills to a piece of writing of essay length.

Be careful to do **exactly** what the question requires and do **all** that it requires.

1 Exactness

For example, in an English literature exam, a passage from a set book is quoted and candidates are asked:

(i) Put into clear modern English the full meaning of the lines:
seld–shown flemens . . . Of Phoebus' burning kisses.

(*6 marks*)

(ii) Comment on the imagery and tone **of this passage**. (*11 marks*)
(From O&CSEB A level English Literature, June 1989)

The answer to (i) must give the **full** meaning and be in **clear, modern** English. The answer to (ii) must **only** comment on the imagery and tone **of this passage**.

As always, take account of the marks available for each part of your answer and assign your time accordingly.

2 Completeness

In one history exam, for example, there is a crucial rubric that applies to **all** its questions:

Candidates should, so far as is possible or appropriate, demonstrate in their answers knowledge and understanding of the prescribed texts.

So, if you are answering the question: 'Who were Cade's supporters in 1450 and why were they in rebellion?' you must prove your knowledge and understanding of the prescribed texts.

3 Give all aspects

Do not leave out any aspect of a question. For example, if answering this question:
'How do you explain the collapse of the Stock Market in October 1987? Should there be stricter market regulation?'
(From O&CSEB A level Economics, June 1989)
you will lose marks if in your answer you forget to discuss the question of stricter market regulation. To avoid this type of oversight, **reread** every essay question carefully half-way through answering it.

● PRACTICAL EXAMS

- read the questions very **carefully**.
- carry out the instructions **accurately**.
- write down **all** observations and readings.
- don't rub out your first readings if you later find they are incorrect: examiners like to see all your results, so cross them out neatly if they are wrong.
- assign your time very carefully between the different parts of a question. Here is one situation from an 'A' level physics exam which shows the importance of this. You have 2¼ hours for four questions, three of which are practical. For each practical question you are allowed 25 minutes with the apparatus and then no further use of it. The examiners envisage the last quarter of an hour as time to **complete** the writing up of your results (i.e. an average of five minutes per practical question). One experiment requires you to do the following:

  (a) carry out the experiment
  (b) tabulate the results and describe carefully how the measurements were made (24 lines are available for this)
  (c) plot the results on a graph
  (d) write up to eight further lines discussing the use of the graph

  Plainly, it is vital for you to obtain as much practice as possible in dividing the available time between the various parts of questions like this.

● SYLLABUSES AND EXAM PAPERS

Get to know, well in advance:
- the name of every syllabus that you are following in each subject.
- the names of the papers you will be taking.
- what sections of each paper apply to you.
- what areas you must study and will be tested on.
- what areas do **not** concern you. You do **not** want to find yourself attempting to answer questions that you have not been prepared for.

Write to your examination board well in advance of the examinations and order several copies of the papers you will be taking. Practise answering whole papers in the time allowed.

Get used to the form of each paper. Be quite clear about such matters as:
- how many sections the paper contains.
- whether there are some optional and some compulsory questions.
- if there is a choice, how many questions you must do.
- the total number of questions in the paper. Does it vary?
- all instructions in each paper.
- typical ways in which marks and time are assigned to questions and parts of questions.

● YOURSELF

To do yourself justice, you need to be mentally fresh and physically rested when you take each paper.

1 Keep some time before and between exams for recreation.

Do not fill all your time with last-minute revision. If you have done what is suggested in this book and revised both throughout your two-year course and for a few months before the exams, then last-minute revision should not be necessary. Approach the exams with an alert and eager mind and you will be able to put in a better performance.

2 Avoid late nights before days on which you have an exam.

It is obvious that a person who is tired is not able to perform at any task as well as one who is rested. Your brain may not be able to make connections and relate points from different topics as successfully when you are tired. After two years of hard work, is it wise to put at risk all your efforts just because, for example, you want to watch a video or stay up late with a friend? If you play tennis or swim or do any other sport, don't give it up as the exams approach. Physical activity will make you feel better about yourself and the exam. If you don't have a sport, try to take fresh air and exercise in some other way, e.g. by walking or cycling.

● TIME DURING AN EXAM PAPER

Before you go into the exam room, work out how much time you will have for each section or question that you must answer. Proceed as follows:

From the total time available for any given paper deduct 5–10 minutes for reading questions and rereading your answers.

If all the sections or questions are likely to be of the same length, then divide the remaining time by the number of sections or questions you must answer. That will give you the amount of time available for each. If some questions or sections are generally longer or more complex than others, take this into account when calculating the time.

Many papers give you advice about how long to spend on a particular question or section. **Follow this advice**. If you have a 1½ hour exam paper and four essay questions to answer out of a choice of 12, for example, how would you divide up your time?

PART 2 THE EXAMINATION ITSELF

● BEFORE YOU START

1 Read the instructions carefully when you have the paper before you.

2 Complete any sections on the front of it if it is a paper of the kind that you have to hand in with your answers written on it.

3 Check that (a) the number of sections and questions you must answer are as expected, and (b) any recommended time is as you expected.

4 When it is time to start, **look** at the clock and quickly **calculate** at what time you should finish each section or main question of the paper.

PRACTICE

Study the front page of the history paper on the next page.

If the exam starts promptly at 10 a.m.:

1 At what time should you finish part 1?

2 At what time should you finish your first essay question?

3 How much time, roughly, is it sensible to allow for each short answer question in part 1?

*4 How much time is recommended for **one** essay question, assuming that each has the same amount of time as the other?*

136

Centre Number	Candidate Number		For Examiner's Use Only
Surname	Initials		
Signature			
Date			

**London and East Anglian Group
for GCSE Examinations**

JUNE 1988

Subject Title	HISTORY — SYLLABUS C: British Economic and Social History
Paper No.	Paper 1
Time allowed	One and three quarter hours

In the boxes above, write your centre number, your candidate number, your surname and your initials, your signature and the date.

This Paper has two Parts, each of which contains twenty Sections:

Part 1 consists of short answer questions. *Look for the TEN Sections for which you have been prepared.* Answer **ALL THREE** questions in each of these ten Sections.

Place bold ticks in the TEN boxes alongside the Sections you have chosen.

☐ Section A: *Agriculture, c.1760–c.1870*

☐ Section B: *Agriculture since c.1870*

☐ Section C: *The Industrial Revolution, c.1760–c.1870*

☐ Section D: *Industrial Developments since c.1870*

☐ Section E: *Population Trends and Urban Society, c.1760–c.1870*

☐ Section F: *Population Trends and Urban Society since c.1870*

☐ Section G: *Transport, c.1760–c.1870*

☐ Section H: *Transport since c.1870*

☐ Section I: *The Working Classes, c.1760–c.1870*

☐ Section J: *Labour in the Economy and Society since c.1870*

☐ Section K: *Social Welfare, c.1760–c.1870*

☐ Section L: *Social Welfare since c.1870*

☐ Section M: *Medicine and Health, c.1760–c.1870*

☐ Section N: *Medicine, Health and Leisure since c.1870*

☐ Section O: *Education, c.1760–c.1870*

☐ Section P: *Education since c.1870*

☐ Section Q: *Women and Society, c.1760–c.1870*

☐ Section R:: *Women and Society c.1870*

☐ Section S: *Trade and Economic Ideas, c.1760–c.1870*

☐ Section T: *Economic Ideas and the British Economy since c.1870*

Your answers must be written in this question booklet.

You are advised to spend about 35 minutes on this Part.

All questions carry equal marks.

Part 2 consists of essay questions. *Answer any TWO questions. The questions you choose must be answered in the separate answer booklet provided. You are advised to spend about 70 minutes on this Part.*

Remember the importance of clear English and orderly presentation in your answers.

MSE 87/0211   7/3/10/27,445/
© 1988 University of London

1

Turn over

● ANSWERING SHORT ANSWER QUESTIONS

For example,

State **two** functions of B.

1 _____

2 _____ (*2 marks*)

1 **Think out** the answer before you write it down, even if you know the answer well. If asked for functions, make sure you give functions.

2 **Work out** a whole sentence in your head before you write down its first word. This will prevent you starting sentences you can't finish.

● ANSWERING ESSAY QUESTIONS

1 **Read all questions**. Do allow yourself enough time to read each question calmly and work out what sort of answer is required. Don't panic and hurriedly opt for a question in which you see a familiar topic intending to write all you know on it.

2 **Decide which questions** to answer.

3 **Plan** each question. Before you write each essay, think and jot down a short list of its main points. Advantages of doing this:

You can

| **relate** ideas from different parts of your notes | **organize** your material | **avoid omitting** points |

4 **Reread** the **question**. Before you write your essay, **check** that your plan meets the requirements of the question.

5 **Write** your essay.

6 **Watch** the time as you write. If short of time, jot down in note form the points which you have not had time to write out in full. This need only take a couple of minutes and could prevent you losing several marks.

● AT THE END OF THE EXAM

1 Read your answers.

2 Check that no question is omitted.

3 Check that no **part** of a question remains unanswered.

4 Check grammar, spelling, punctuation.
Good English makes a good impression.
Good impressions earn marks.

ANSWERS

Practice on page 130
1 Four examples.

Practice on page 136
1 10.35 a.m.
2 11.10 a.m., allowing five minutes for reading and choosing questions and 30 minutes for answering one.
3 Allow one minute for each (10 × 3 questions). This leaves you five minutes spare.
4 If you have 70 minutes for two questions and if you allow five minutes for reading and choosing questions and five minutes at the end of reading over your work, you have 30 minutes to plan and write each essay.

Subject-Specific Skills
Studying economics and business studies

● THE GCSE SKILLS REQUIRED

- to recall knowledge and use it in various ways.
- to explain technical terms, ideas and simple theories.
- to find and choose between differing sources.
- to distinguish between evidence and opinion, facts and value judgements.
- to select, analyse, interpret and use data.
- to make reasoned judgements and communicate them in an accurate and logical manner.

● GCSE ECONOMICS

You need to develop a knowledge and understanding of:

- **scarcity** as an economic concept.
- main aspects of the **British economy**

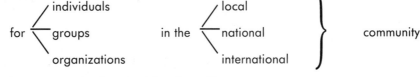

- major issues of UK **economic policy**.
- basic economic **terminology** and elementary **theory**.

You need to develop these skills:
- to use the **methods** of economic analysis.
- to **apply** them correctly in particular situations.
- basic economic **numeracy** and **literacy**.

● GCSE BUSINESS STUDIES

You need to develop a knowledge and understanding of:

- the business **environment**.
- how **changes** in this environment influence businesses.
- the main **organizations** inside and outside business and how they influence business objectives, decisions and activities.
- the **roles** and **purposes** of business activity in both public and private sectors.
- **competition** and **monopoly**.
- the **organization**, **finance** and **operation** of businesses and commercial institutions.
- the **regulation** of their relations with other organizations.
- the **world** of **work** and how **cooperation** is an essential part of it.
- business **concepts**, **language** and ways of **making decisions**.
- **innovation** and **change**: their nature and significance in business activities.

It is important to develop the skill of working with others inside and outside the classroom.

● COURSE WORK

For general aspects of coursework and projects, see Chapter 13.

1 Specifically economics points:

- you must understand and use **economic terms**.
- you must use them **relevantly**.
- you must **apply** them to particular aspects of your study.
- it is a good idea to include one or more such terms in the **title** of your project.
- bring them into your introduction.
- refer to them in the course of your project.

- the most important terms are: scarcity
                              choice
                              opportunity cost
                              interdependence
                              efficiency

Other terms are:

price	resources	income
market	locations	competition
demand	production	private sector
costs/benefits	sales	local economy

2 Business studies points:

You should:

- **choose** a **topic** which is on the syllabus and which enables you to show your understanding of business.
- give particular attention to **searching** for and obtaining information. Visits to organizations must be very carefully prepared if full advantage is to be obtained.
- **choose** from all that you have gathered what is **relevant** to your project.
- **interpret** what you have selected.
- present your work **in business terms**, using figures, tables, diagrams, etc, as appropriate, to support your text.

● 'A' LEVEL

- the subject content will be more difficult.
- there will be more emphasis on the 'higher order' skills of **theoretical analysis** and **evaluation**.
- knowledge of subject-specific **sources of information** and **methods of enquiry** assume greater importance.

● STUDY AIDS

Computers

These can help you as follows:

1 Through data bases. These are collections of data about a particular topic. Such information may be useful to you. The main advantage of a data base is its speec Examples of data bases:
   (a) the indexes to books in a library
   (b) television teletext services, e.g. Ceefax and Oracle, which provide information on travel, sport, weather, etc
   (c) British Telecom's Prestel, providing thousands of pages of specialist information

2 Through programs that enable you to create your own data base. A group of you on a coursework project could **store** the results of your investigation on a computer disc:
   (a) the stored information can be **retrieved** later
   (b) the data base can **sort** information. This can save time, e.g. when analysing the results of a questionnaire

Wordprocessors

1 Can store information for you.

2 Can print information (as many copies as you need).

3 Enable you to edit information (i.e. change it, update it, rearrange it, correct it).

●EXAMS

The following question types may be used:

(a) essay, see page 134
(b) data/stimulus response, see page 131
(c) multiple choice, see page 130
(d) case study, see below
(e) assessment may also include coursework assignments and a project, see Chapter 13

Case studies

1 These are questions based on a text, diagram or tables.

2 This data may be issued about six weeks before the exam, giving you time to stud the material, its theme, and its implications.

3 In the exam, the case study is presented again with questions for you to answer.

4 A case study may be based on a particular theme such as the development of a business over a period of years. Questions might deal with the finance of the business, its management structure, customers' requirements, the recruitment of employees.

5 Your answers must show that you are applying to the case study situation knowledge obtained during your course of study. This means that you may draw on subject knowledge from outside the case study material. Opportunities to do this occur when you are asked for advice on a given situation or your assessment of a problem.

● DISTANCE LEARNING

This means a written correspondence course by post. It may be supported by radio and television programmes and computer-assisted learning.

Disadvantage: lack of stimulus through little contact with teachers and other students.

Therefore some courses provide **telephone** contact with tutors, and **weekend** or **holiday** schools.

Advantages:

1 Correspondence course material is available to students everywhere.

2 Time spent in travelling to classes can be used for study.

3 You progress at your own pace.

4 Your tutor plans the course to ensure complete coverage.

5 Regular feedback is provided through comments on your work.

6 You can combine part-time study with a job.

Studying English

● GENERAL SKILLS FOR ENGLISH

1 Reading

Means understanding and responding to all types of writing as well as obtaining information for study purposes.

Therefore read as widely as possible: guide books, consumer reports, textbooks, instructions and manuals, brochures, forms, contracts, newspapers and magazines as well as novels, plays and poems.

2 Writing

Means organizing and expressing meaning in written language, suiting style to audience and purpose.

Therefore for each piece of writing, **know** your audience and purpose. Attempt a wide range of styles: notes, diaries, personal and formal letters, narratives, reports, pamphlets, reviews, essays, advertisements, newspaper articles, biography, autobiography, poems, stories and playscripts.

3 Listening and speaking

Means understanding what is said, expressing oneself effectively in a variety of activities, suiting style to audience and purpose.

Therefore participate in varied activities with varied groups: question arguments and evidence, present group views, read aloud prepared pieces varying your timing, stress and intonation, give talks, join in debates. Listen to recordings of your own speech and that of others: improve your performance.

141

4 Presentation

Means presenting finished work appropriately, clearly and attractively after checking for misspelling, bad punctuation and other mechanical errors.

Therefore have neat writing and layout. Improve spelling: use 'look, cover, write, check' method to learn new words. Learn to use dictionaries, thesauruses, spelling checkers. Become interested in words, their derivations and spelling rules.

 **SKILLS FOR GCSE**

Coursework

1 English

Writing: personal, imaginative, narrative, informative, argument.
Reading: **understanding** literary and non-literary material,
responding to reading material, covering at least one whole work. If the course is 100 per cent coursework (such courses will end in 1994), comprehension will be tested under controlled conditions without assistance.

2 English literature

Understanding and **responding** to a whole text in at least two of the three genres of prose, poetry and drama:
Showing evidence of wider reading and response in all three genres;
Responding to unseen material, usually under controlled conditions (one coursework piece);
Completing one other coursework piece under controlled conditions.

3 Oral

You must have participated in a variety of speaking and listening situations involving individual, pair and group work, including formal talks and discussions.

Examination

1 English

Though Boards differ slightly, all exam papers test understanding and synthesis. An extract has to be understood and you give either short answers or respond with a longer piece in a given style (letter, report, review). In addition, a piece of factual writing is usually required, produced by drawing material from a variety of sources (e.g. statistical material, pictures, writing). This tests synthesis and the ability to write for a given audience.

2 English literature

You need a **full knowledge** of the set of texts: plot, character, theme. If you are able, achieve an awareness of style and how it is achieved. Questions will look for your **personal response** to these aspects. An ability to communicate an informed and sensitive response, often by empathy with one of the characters, is highly valued.

 **SKILLS FOR 'A' LEVEL LITERATURE**

General skills

Exams test:

- **knowledge** of set books and the circumstances in which they were written.
- **understanding** of them at surface and underlying levels.
- ability to describe **literary effects** and how they are achieved.
- the making of **value judgements** supported by details.
- awareness of **literary tradition** and the place of a text within or outside it.
- **personal response**.
- the **writing** of clear, concise and relevant English.

Coursework

1 Provides opportunities for responses that need more time than exams allow. You must show breadth and balance in both choice of texts and types of response. Your folder will include traditional essays and more imaginative approaches, e.g. letters written between characters, extra scenes, alternative endings, extracts from characters' secret diaries, key scenes rewritten from the perspective of a different character, notes for a performance of a scene or poem, a drawing or other graphic response, creative writing arising out of the themes in a text, comparisons of film and book, pastiche, reworking of a text in a different genre . . .

2 Provides opportunities to redraft (see page 144).

3 Usually requires an extended essay, often a comparison of several texts, the work of a particular writer or within one genre. Wide reading is essential as well as basing generalizations on evidence drawn from it.

142

Examinations

These elements are included:

1 Critical appreciation (i.e. commentary and analysis): you respond to a poem or prose extracts and judge their worth, analysing theme, diction, imagery, form and effect with supporting evidence. To master this you will need:
    (a) frequent timed practice with feedback from teachers
    (b) wide and varied reading throughout the whole of English literature

2 Set texts: read and reread set texts frequently (see below).

3 Timed conditions: these require quick and efficient planning, clarity and conciseness. Recommended planning time:
    (a) five minutes for a 45 minute answer on a set text
    (b) much longer for critical appreciation, e.g. up to 30 minutes for reading, thinking and planning a one hour 10 minute answer.

It is essential to practise timed answers throughout your course.

● THE DIFFERING APPROACH TO GCSE AND 'A' LEVEL

	GCSE	A level
Number of texts	Not so many	More texts
Level of texts	Less difficult	More advanced
Aspects of text	Plot, theme, character	As GCSE and (a) social and historical context, (b) different interpretations of a text
Comparison	Within a text	Between whole texts, and therefore consideration of genre
Writing	Moderate length	Longer pieces, ability to handle technical vocabulary of literary criticism with ease
		Extended study/ study of non-fiction } some syllabuses
	Personal response	Personal response informed by very wide reading in all genres

● READING SKILLS FOR THE STUDY OF LITERATURE

1 Read a text first and fully for a general appreciation of it.

2 Read a text several times more, each time for a particular **purpose**, e.g.:
    (a) to complete your understanding of a complex plot
    (b) to study the interaction of particular characters
    (c) to become familiar with style or mood

3 More able 'A' level candidates can reread from different **positions**, e.g.:
    (a) from a feminist viewpoint
    (b) from a Marxist viewpoint

● ENGLISH LITERATURE REFERENCE TEXTS

Use:

● a dictionary of literary terms.
● *The Penguin Guide to English Literature* (one volume per literary 'period'). This provides the social and historical information needed at 'A' level.
● *Rereading Literature* by Hackman and Marshall, Hodder and Stoughton, 1990.
● collections of critical essays, e.g. the Macmillan *Casebook* series. They are interesting, but mustn't supplant your own thinking.

Avoid:

● published 'notes'. These are usually limited and liable to be used as a substitute for genuine thought and personal response.

● ENGLISH-SPECIFIC WRITING SKILLS

Personal, imaginative and creative writing.

143

DRAFTING AND REDRAFTING

Drafting is crucially important to the writing process. It is a series of steps leading to a finished piece of work.

1 Drafting

Getting first ideas down, in whatever form.

2 Redrafting

Shaping and structuring the raw material, taking account of audience and purpose.

3 Rereading and revising

Checking and removing ambiguities, irrelevancies, imprecision.

4 Proof reading

Dealing with such matters as spelling and punctuation.

Drafting enables you to demonstrate your best work. It is the single most important step forward in the assessment of English for 20 years. Make the most of it.

EXAM USE OF TEXTS AND NOTES

There are three types of literature examination:

1 Blind exams

No texts are allowed in the exam room. You will need to (a) learn quotations by heart as you study, (b) revise them frequently and (c) frequently use them in examination answer practice.

2 Plain text exams

The text is allowed, but no introductions, end notes or marginal notes. Rote learning is not necessary, but the text must be thoroughly known to avoid wasting time searching for a 'useful bit'. You may have to relate a specific extract to the text as a whole. Lengthy quotation is pointless.

3 Open text exams

The text and any printed notes, introduction and critical essays it may contain are allowed. You are also allowed notes you have made in the margin while studying, but not notes on separate pieces of paper. Make as many notes as you can on the text itself while studying. Become thoroughly familiar with the text, too. You will have to relate a specific extract to the text as a whole. Personal response will be highly rewarded, but do not just write out chunks of your own notes: use them as a source of ideas. Lengthy quotation is pointless here, too.

COMMON ERRORS IN EXAMS

1 Bad planning of answers. Planning is expected and rewarded if well done.

2 Relying on quantity, not quality. At 'A' level, some chief examiners look for answers of only two to three sides of A4.

3 Not referring to the text in support of points. But don't overquote: quote briefly and to the point—three lines is usually the maximum.

4 Poor expression, faulty punctuation and spelling. It is especially important to make a good impression in these areas at 'A' level.

5 Retelling the story. No literature question requires this: it can never show a personal response.

6 Using critical terms without understanding them.

7 Explaining at length in critical terms what a text lacks.

Studying geography

● GENERAL SKILLS

1 Enquiry skills
You should be able to undertake an individual or small group investigation into a geographical topic in the form of a problem-solving exercise. You should support this with fieldwork and the use of a variety of secondary sources.

2 Fieldwork techniques
You need to be able to:
- observe and record features outside the classroom.
- use sampling techniques relating to both the physical and human landscapes.
- select diagrams to present the information collected.
- evaluate this information.

3 Secondary sources
You should be able to:
- extract relevant information from secondary sources such as visual, written and oral sources.
- analyse and interpret geographical data using such facilities as spreadsheets and data handling software.
- analyse and interpret data concerned with employment and tourism.

4 Maps and diagrams
You need to be able to:
- use grid references.
- follow a route on an Ordnance Survey map.
- plan routes and measure distances using maps of appropriate scales.
- use compass bearings to follow a route.
- design a layout.
- identify features on aerial photographs.
- use latitude and longitude to find places on atlas maps.
- draw cross sections of small scale features using your own field measurements.
- extract information from thematic maps as an aid to selecting the best site for an enterprise.
- draw an annotated sketch to record and interpret a landscape.
- measure and record weather conditions using simple instruments.
- intepret synoptic charts and satellite images of cloud patterns.
- use systems to interpret geographical relationships.
- draw annotated sketch maps to show relationships between physical and human features.
- identify and interpret relief, settlement and communication patterns using maps.

● SKILLS FOR GCSE

You will receive marks for:
- recall of specific facts.
- understanding and applying these facts.
- skills.
- understanding values relevant to geography.

Knowledge of facts is essential, but many examination boards award most of the available marks for skills and understanding and applying the facts.

In addition to the more general skills of finding and selecting relevant information and writing it up concisely, you will need these more specifically geographical skills:

1 Mapping skills
Drawing maps which highlight what is relevant and exclude other material.

2 Geographical skills
Interpreting and drawing line, bar and scatter graphs and other graphic devices.

3 Diagram skills
Producing the relevant, annotated diagram to support a written explanation.

4 Photographic interpretation skills
Selecting and emphasizing evidence that is relevant in support of your viewpoint.

5 Sketching skills
Producing a good annotated field sketch.

6 Fieldwork skills
Collecting and processing raw data from outside the classroom. This will normally involve:
  (a) choosing the general topic, posing a question to be answered or hypothesis to be tested
  (b) obtaining the necessary background material for the general topic
  (c) working out the best methods of data collection in the field
  (d) collecting the data accurately, sorting and refining it
  (e) analyzing and processing all the data, both primary and secondary
  (f) interpreting the data in the light of the original question or hypothesis

Coursework will probably involve working as part of a team (for data collection) and any work will need to be closely related to assessment criteria.

● SKILLS FOR 'A' LEVEL

You will need to:
● greatly extend your research skills.
● read well beyond the basic texts issued by your school or college, including magazine and newspaper articles; watch relevant TV programmes.
● achieve a deeper understanding of what it means to study geography.
● establish links between points, e.g.:

  (a) between points you may have learnt in separate parts of your course
  (b) between physical and human aspects of the environment
This question illustrates the need for such links:

How far is the transport network more closely related to the distribution of population than to relief and drainage? Give examples from one or more developed countries to illustrate your answer.

● make judgements about problems or issues and support your viewpoint with evidence, e.g.:

Examine the problems of siting new airports in developed countries.

To answer such a question, you have to **think out** the factors that are **common** to a variety of countries, **state** them as general points and **support** these general points with evidence from specific countries.
● evaluate source material, consider conflicting evidence, make up your own mind and defend your position with evidence.
● be able to understand and discuss models and concepts using appropriate terms.
● be able to understand and discuss processes and changes over time.

It is not enough to possess factual knowledge: you must be able to **use** it to make a point and argue a case.

● ACCURACY IN MAPPING

1 Every map must have a scale (even if only approximate) and a 'north point'.

2 Every map must be neat.

3 Any colours or symbols you use must be identified in a key.

4 You should print place names and position them carefully to avoid obscuring other essential data.

5 Each map should be designed for a specific purpose.

6 You will probably need to adapt any generalized map you have learnt so that it suits the particular purpose of the examination question.

7 You must ensure that a map used as part of an exam answer is totally relevant to that answer and you **must refer to it in your written text**: it is there to aid your answer, not as mere decoration.

8 You may use annotations to help emphasize key features which have a direct relationship to your written answer.

9 You may similarly annotate diagrams and photographs that support a written answer.

146

● TIMING THE EXAM

1 Divide the available time carefully between the questions you decide to answer.

2 In a four-question paper of three hours, allot:
   (a) 10 minutes to studying the paper and making your choices
   (b) 50 minutes for your first answer
   (c) 40 minutes only for each of your other answers

3 Be strict about adhering to these times.

4 Do your **best** answer **first**: it is good for your morale and will maximize marks.

5 Do your **weakest** answer **last**: if time is short, minimum marks are lost.

6 If you are running seriously out of time, you are probably including either **irrelevant** material or **unnecessary** detail.

This comes about through the poor distribution of time:	one excellent answer one reasonable answer one below average answer one barely started answer	yielding a **much lower** mark than you are capable of.

● INDIVIDUAL EXAM QUESTIONS

1 Plan each answer, jotting down:
   (a) introduction, e.g. method to be used in answering the question
   (b) main lines of your developing argument and supporting hard facts
   (c) ideas for sketch maps and diagrams
   (d) conclusion: **not** for repeating an earlier point. It should be a final, definitive, clinching statement that really answers the question in a sentence

2 As you write:
   (a) **think out** each sentence before writing it down
   (b) **discard** any irrelevant material or 'padding'
   (c) from time to time **look again** at the question and your plan and at what you have written so far. Ask yourself 'Am I straying?' The ideal answer should be a short, concise piece of prose in which every word tells
   (d) illustrate every major point you make with an actual example in its regional setting, especially in physical geography
   (e) avoid writing in an abstract vein using unexplained terms and ill-digested jargon
   (f) where possible, write in terms of your own personal experience and fieldwork

● 'ISSUES BASED' EXAMS

1 Study carefully all the resources supplied to build up the maximum background information.

2 Consider carefully all aspects of the issues raised.

3 Prepare a closely reasoned argument, making full use of the relevant evidence provided.

● SPOTTING QUESTIONS TARGETED AT MORE/LESS ABLE STUDENTS

1 Some questions require a specific approach and treatment (**specific** questions).

2 Some questions are more generally phrased (**general** questions).

3 **Specific** questions are easier than **general** ones. You can recognize them by such directive phrases as **analyze**, **compare**, **discuss the ways in which** . . .

4 **More structured** questions, where there is greater guidance as to what is required, are also easier than general questions.

5 **General** questions may consist of a quotation followed by just the word **discuss**.

These tend to be answered by:
   (a) very able candidates who can appreciate the question's implications
   (b) poor candidates seizing upon such questions since they imagine, wrongly, that they do not call for hard facts

6 Choose appropriately according to your ability.

147

Studying history

● ACQUIRING KNOWLEDGE

You will learn historical information partly from **primary** (first-hand) sources and partly from **secondary** (second-hand) sources. Primary sources include photographs, drawings, diaries, letters, wills, statistics and other documents written at about the time of an event. Secondary sources are usually books or articles based on primary sources. They are the result of **selection** from primary sources and **interpretation** of them.

You will mainly learn by **reading**. But remember to use, carefully, film, video, drama, museums, visits to historical sites, appreciation of artefacts, and other means. **How** you read is all-important.

1 **Understand** the text. If you can't make full sense of it, note important ideas, movements and people that you need to read more about elsewhere.

2 Be **curious** to find out more; have an enquiring attitude.

3 Be **critical**. Look out for contradictory points and gaps in evidence.

4 **Relate** one aspect with another. See how various pieces of information fit together to make a coherent picture of the past.

● RETENTION OF KNOWLEDGE

You will remember history better if you:
● **revise** from time to time to keep information fresh in your mind.
● take an **interest** in the subject: you can't forget things that really interest you.
● do **background reading**. Read about the farming, costumes, religion, music, travel, technology, etc, of your period. This creates a framework to lock your historical facts into. Books on such topics will also mention historical figures and events, thus 'revising' them for you. A **sense of historical period** will be an asset to you as a historian.

● STUDYING HISTORY

Syllabuses identify some important considerations:

Cause and consequence

1 Distinguish an **immediate** cause (or **occasion**) from **long-term** causes. An immediate cause might be an otherwise unimportant event that triggered a war.

2 Appreciate that two factors may not be independent, but **related** causes. Cause can be complex.

3 Evaluate the **relative importance** of various causes. This is particularly important for 'A' level students. It is no use simply memorizing five causes when questions are framed like this:

How far was X responsible for Y?

Was the Thirty Years War **primarily** a war of religion?

To what extent . . . ?

With **what** success . . . ?

4 Distinguish **immediate** consequences, **longer-term** effects and **wider** ramifications.

Change and continuity

1 Change is **not** always **linear**; does not always proceed one step at a time at a constant rate. It can be complex.

2 Change is **not** always **progressive**: there may be steps backwards.

3 Change need not be **dramatic** (e.g. as a result of an actual revolution). It can **evolve** gradually.

4 Continuity: be aware how institutions, customs, attitudes, etc, have their origins in the past. See links between the present and the past.

Similarity and difference

These involve making comparisons.

Be **complete** in your comparisons. If, for example, you have to compare two reigns, (let us say reign A and reign B), you will have to think of the various aspects you will consider, e.g. law and order, foreign policy, economic management, etc. You must, then, discuss law and order under reign A **and** under reign B, foreign policy under reign A **and** under reign B, etc. Make it clear that you are comparing: use expressions like **whereas**, **however**, **more** . . . **than** . . . , **like** . . . , **unlike** . . . .

USING HISTORICAL EVIDENCE

1 Bias

Since every source that is written or drawn by a person is also a selection and interpretation of the facts, it may contain a degree of bias. To assess this possibility, consider together:

(a) who the writer is and all you know about this person
(b) the actual material itself

2 Reliability

A text is reliable if you have confidence that what is says is **true**.

3 Accuracy

A text is accurate if it is true **in detail**.

4 Usefulness

A text is useful if you can obtain historical insights from it, even if its surface information is not reliable. For example, if a Soviet Prime Minister claims that western banks (not named) are flooding Soviet society with millions of rouble bank notes in order to undermine the economy, you may decide that this claim is not reliable. However, you may find it a useful **insight** into the attitudes of some senior Soviet officials.

5 Causes of unreliability

- self-interest: a memoir-writer may deliberately blame others for his faults while in office.
- prejudice: the writer may be known to have set views.
- propaganda: to promote a national or partisan cause or policy.
- emotion: the feelings of a letter-writer may distort his perception of events.
- error: even official documents can be in error or not represent exactly what they claim.

6 Signs of unreliability

See 'Bias and balance' on page 72. Look particularly for:

- – sweeping, unsupported generalizations
- – gaps in evidence
- – emotive language
- – suspect figures

When you discuss sources, you should do so in terms of the points listed above, supporting **your** statements with sound evidence.

EMPATHY

When you write with empathy you write:

(a) about a **specific** historical situation
(b) from the viewpoint of **other** people, in **another** culture, at **another** time and, possibly, in **another** place

- you **recreate** their attitudes and beliefs.
- you **understand** their motivation.
- you **estimate** how they would have reacted.
- your writing **reflects** the fact that **not all** people in a given past society would have reacted in the same way to a specific set of circumstances.

You can only do this if:

- you **understand** the cultures and circumstances of people in other societies. You must **show** your ability to do this.
- you **know** enough about the people, the historical background, the facts.

Your answers must be rooted in historical evidence. They should **not** be simply **imaginary** ('made-up', fictitious). But they should be **imaginative**: showing a sensitive appreciation of the realities of other times and other peoples. You would, of course, measure them by the standards of their day, not in the light of present-day perspectives.

PROJECTS

Choice of topic

- its scope should be limited.
- primary sources should be available. Why not visit a local museum, record office, public library, and/or archives and see what topics they have material on before deciding your topic?
- travelling should be kept to a minimum.
- ensure there are no obstacles to your investigation.
- it should be enjoyable to research and interesting to you and anyone reading it.

Consulting local documents

1 Take: pen, pocket-sized notebook, pencil, pencil-sharpener, camera, clipboard if sketching, portable tape recorder (for interviews and for your own observations).

2 Ask permission: do this when necessary, e.g. for photographs, always for recording interviews, when entering private property.

3 Plan: think ahead of all you will need to do when visiting a particular place. Avoid having to revisit it unnecessarily.

For other aspects of projects see Chapter 13.

ARGUMENT

You will often need to assemble and assess evidence and argue a case. Read page 99 on writing involving argument. In particular:

- assess **all** the relevant evidence, weighing up points on both (or all) sides of a question.
- decide the stance that you take on the issue and how you will deal with all the evidence—your judgement of the relative strength, weakness, importance of each point is crucial. Your position should be a balanced one.
- present your discussion in an organized way, dealing, where appropriate, with opposing points in pairs or groups.
- reach a clear conclusion.

PREPARING FOR THE EXAM

Follow the advice in Chapters 14 and 15. Also:

- obtain past papers.
- practise making plans for answers to questions.
- include in your plans your judgements of the relative importance of events/causes/consequences, etc.
- think how you can make use of **what you know** to answer specific questions.

Learning a modern language

THE VITAL SKILLS

1 Make **listening** and **speaking** just as important as **reading** and **writing**.

2 Understand clearly and use correctly the grammar and structures of the language.

3 Aim to 'think' in the foreign language: to respond **directly**, at least in everyday conversation.

4 Practise using the language as much as you can in a wide variety of situations.

5 Find out from your examining group or board what is required at your level (basic, extended, 'A') in terms of such features as essential words and grammatical structures. For example, in French the past historic may be needed only in reading at the extended level, while the imperfect may be expected in any test at any level.

6 Focus your study on requirements like these.

Contact with foreign speakers

1 Have as much contact as possible with the target language.

2 The diagram below shows ways of experiencing it, especially through contact with native speakers.

Exchange visits between your class and a class in the foreign country

Visit the country on holiday

Stay with a family in the foreign country

Read lots of simple books & magazines in the foreign language

Arrange to

Sing songs in the foreign language

Watch films (e.g. on TV) in the foreign language

Listen to radio broadcasts and make recordings

Listen to any tapes you can get hold of in the foreign language

Join in any relevant twinning activities in your town

Write to a penfriend in the foreign country

Join, or start, a French/German/Spanish club in your school

3 When on visits abroad, be patient, positive and persistent: don't be afraid of making mistakes, have a shot at speaking, ask people to speak more slowly, deliberately add to your collection of conversational phrases.

4 When abroad, take in language around you, e.g. advertisements, posters, the media; if in an English-speaking group, keep to a minimum your chatting with others in the group; bring home magazines and other reading material.

5 After a visit, keep up a correspondence with a host family: exchange magazines and other printed material.

Reading

1 GCSE tests usually require you to extract information from a wide variety of written/printed language.

2 Read letters, menus, timetables, newspaper articles, notices, leaflets, etc.

3 In addition to what your teacher provides, read whatever you can get hold of.

4 After reading something, work out what you might be asked about it in an examination. Note useful words and phrases.

5 Constant reading of simple readers will increase your command of the language and your confidence.

6 If necessary, ask for more readers or buy some yourself after taking advice.

Listening

1 Many types of question may be used to test your understanding of announcements, instructions, monologues, dialogues, radio extracts and other everyday items. At the extended level you maybe asked to draw conclusions or identify emotions and ideas.

2 Use mainly class material, but also record parts of foreign news bulletins when you know their content through English news programmes.

3 Use TV language teaching programmes at the appropriate level.

Speaking

1 Aim to communicate; do not be put off by the possibility of making mistakes.

2 Learn, by frequent use, question and answer patterns.

3 Imitate intonation and stress patterns for statements, questions, exclamations.

4 Follow up class work through conversations with friends and at home.

Writing

1 Basic level writing tasks vary between the examining groups, but all require such simple communication or response tasks as shopping lists, messages, postcards, simple letters. You should communicate accurately the information you are asked to. Do exactly what the question asks, not omitting points that are specified.

2 Extended level tasks may include a piece of continuous writing, often between 100 and 150 words, e.g. a letter or narrative account in response to a situation or document. Keep strictly to the terms of the question.

3 Learn everyday ways of asking for and giving information, e.g. In French, **est-ce que** in front of a statement turns it into a question, use **quand** to ask **when**? List expressions, in French or another language, for asking **where**?, **who**?, **(at) what time**?, **how**?, **how much**?, **how many**?, **which**?, **which one**? Work out short answers to such questions. Check if your syllabus requires full sentences.

4 **Points to check in French:**
   Verbs
   (a) right tense? (if asked to write a note saying you **are spending** a week at your brother's don't say 'I **spent** a week. . .')
   (b) right person? (right verb for the subject?)
   (c) right form? (is the verb regular or irregular?)
   (d) in the perfect tense is the auxiliary **avoir** or **être**?. Should any past participles agree?

   Nouns
   (a) right gender?
   (b) if plural, regular or irregular?

   Pronouns
   (a) right word for **you**?
   (b) object pronouns in the right order?

   Adjectives
   (a) do they agree with the noun they describe?
   (b) any irregular feminines or plurals?

   Constructions
   right links between main and dependent verbs? e.g. Je **vais voir** ce film (direct link); Nous avons essayé de nager (linked by **de**).

5 **Points to check in German:**
   Verbs
   (a) right tense?
   (b) right person? (right form for subject?)
   (c) right form? (check whether strong or weak, regular or irregular)
   (d) in perfect tense, is the auxiliary **haben** or **sein**?

152

Nouns
(a) right gender?
(b) right form, if plural?

Pronouns
(a) right word for **you**?
(b) right form for case and gender/plural?

Cases
(a) right case after prepositions? e.g. **Er schwimmt** im **Wasser, Er ist ins Wasser gefallen**
(b) right case for subject, direct object, indirect object? e.g. **Meine Mutter hat dem alten Mann einen Kuchen gegeben**

Adjectives
(a) right set of adjective endings where the adjective goes with a noun?
(b) right endings for gender/number and case of adjectives?

Word order
(a) subject/verb inversion where necessary?
(b) participles in the right place?
(c) infinitives in the right position?
(d) have I moved the main verb to the end in a subordinate clause?
(e) are any direct and indirect objects in the right order?
(f) are adverbs and adverbial phrases in the right order?

6 Limit yourself to language that you know to be correct.

7 Avoid thinking out what you want to say in English and then translating it. Ask yourself what you have learnt that will fit this situation.

8 Learn all the ways of beginning and ending letters.

9 If your language is not French or German, make up a list of points to check.

'A' AND 'AS' LEVEL SKILLS

Check the requirements of your board.

Reading

1 Exams differ widely, e.g. questions on a long passage or summary of all or part of an extract. Usual sources are newspapers, magazines, publicity materials, letters, guides and brochures.

2 Collect as much material of these types as you can; persuade your school to obtain them for the library; check what is in your public library.

3 Ensure that a good part of your reading is analytical. Choose likely texts. What are the essential points? Is the reasoning valid? Is there bias? Imagine likely comprehension questions.

4 Read widely; look for new expressions or familiar ones with new meanings.

5 'Authentik' publications are useful: up to date, interesting, including media extracts, games and exercises.

Translation into English (some boards)

1 Understand and express fully and accurately the meaning of the original.

2 Do so in natural English, using an appropriate style.

3 Do not leave gaps: always have a try.

4 Use what you know (especially from the context) to work out what you don't know.

Listening

1 Testing is mainly of understanding of recorded native speakers.

2 You normally show your understanding in English, sometimes through objective tests.

3 Use 'Authentik' cassettes (see above).

4 Record, in a planned progression, news bulletins, forecasts, sports reports, etc.

5 Identify the main points in your recordings, pick out detailed facts and figures, work out likely questions and find answers.

6 Play back your recordings repeatedly: gain competence and confidence.

Speaking

1 Marks for the oral test have increased in recent years.

2 Board requirements differ and may include: role play, negotiation, discussion of a contemporary topic based on an extract. For some tasks there are several days in which to prepare. Some discussions relate to the candidate's personal interests.

3 Know your board's requirements.

4 Marks are awarded for fluency, accuracy, getting your ideas across, explaining yourself convincingly.

5 Plentiful live practice is essential.

6 Consciously collect a stock of conventional expressions, styles and gambits through listening to recordings of the foreign language.

Writing

1 Test may be continuous writing in response to an essay title or written or visual material.

2 A **use of language** test may require you to show your knowledge of the way the target language operates.

3 You may have to translate into the foreign language.

4 You need a thorough knowledge of the grammar, syntax and constructions of the language you are learning.

5 Where possible, choose topics for which your command of the language is strongest.

6 Avoid working out your text in English first and then translating it.

7 If you don't know a word, think of a paraphrase. For example, if you don't know 'make-up', use 'face powder' or 'lipstick'.

8 Use the checks listed for GCSE (p. 152), with these additions:
French:
Verbs
(a) in compound tenses, is the auxiliary **avoir** or **être**?
(b) are any subjunctives needed?

Adjectives
any special sound masculine forms e.g. '**un nouvel auteur**.'?

Pronouns
do all possessive and demonstrative pronouns agree with the nouns for which they stand?

Constructions
any tricky objects?

German:
Verbs
(a) in compound tenses, is the auxiliary **haben** or **sein**?
(b) are any subjunctives needed?

Pronouns
are all possessive and demonstrative pronouns in the right gender or number and case?

Cases
any verbs governing the dative?

Word order
look out for pairs of infinitives in a subordinate clause.

9 If your language is not French or German, make a list of points to check.

154

USING A DICTIONARY

1 If using a bilingual dictionary, it **must** include a **range** of meanings and usages for each entry.

2 Learn thoroughly how to use it, especially how it indicates parts of speech. Know all its signs, symbols and abbreviations.

3 Monolingual dictionaries help you (a) to cut out English as an intermediary, (b) to explain things in the target language (through familiarity with the methods of definition), (c) to appreciate nuances of meaning.

4 Good monolingual dictionaries provide synonyms, antonyms and examples of usage.

LEARNING AND EXTENDING USE OF WORDS

1 The best way to learn words is in groups that are related **either** by form, e.g. **battre**, **se battre**, **la batterie**, **abattre**, etc, *or* by theme, e.g. travel and transport words.

2 Learn vocabulary 'little and often', not large quantities at one attempt.

3 When learning a new noun, learn its gender and plural form; learn the construction taken by French verbs, any special usages of German verbs.

4 Wide experience of the language is a very important means of extending vocabulary.

FINALLY

1 Practice in using language is the best way of revising it.

2 Skill in using language must be backed up by thorough knowledge of grammar, usages, constructions and vocabulary.

3 Use revision cards for grammar and vocabulary. For example, by learning the principal parts of a French verb, you can work out all its tenses:
pouvoir—to be able

pres. indic. je peux (puis-je?)
tu peux
il peut
nous pouvons
vous pouvez
ils peuvent
future je pourrai, etc
past part. pu (aux. avoir)
past hist. je pus, etc
pres. subj. je puisse, etc

4 Be resourceful in exams: there are no marks for writing or saying nothing.

5 Learn how to ask for a question to be repeated, for someone to speak more slowly, for the meaning of a word to be explained.

6 If you don't know a word, e.g. father-in-law, car park, to plant, think of an alternative way of expressing the idea.

Studying science

● **SCIENCE SKILLS**

Develop your — investigative skills
— understanding of science

by systematic — investigation
— experimentation

When you investigate, you try to find out the answers to problems. You often need to suggest ideas or make guesses or suggestions. These then need to be tested by suitable experiment. Testing your ideas will let you learn more about the world we live in and scientific ways of working.

This diagram and the points below it give some of the skills of investigation.

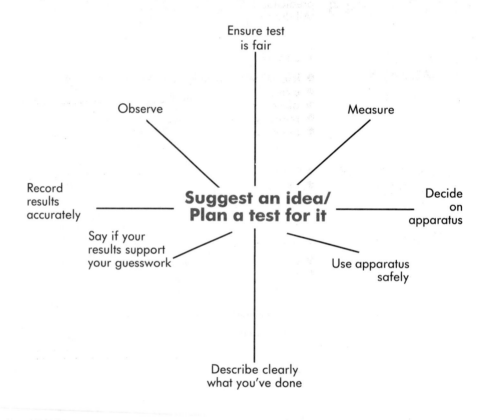

Further aspects of these skills:

- use concepts you know to solve practical everyday problems.
- follow instructions carefully.
- form hypotheses.
- be ready to change your investigation plan.
- when observing, read instrument scales accurately.
- decide on number, range and accuracy of measurements.
- use any appopriate data.
- consider which variables to control or vary and select apparatus accordingly.
- choose and use more complex apparatus to improve measurements.
- present results clearly, appropriately, logically.
- use appropriate graphical representation of data.
- use mathematical relationships where appropriate.
- translate information from one form to another.
- say if results are reliable; if not, take appropriate action.
- notice mistakes, errors.

- see patterns, relationships.
- draw conclusions from experimental evidence.
- make predictions.
- use a computer or word processor if helpful.
- write a full account of the investigation.
- use more and more technical vocabulary when reporting findings and conclusions.

Skills of investigation can be grouped under these five headings:

1 Planning an investigation 2 Carrying it out
3 Observing 4 Inferring (applying your mind to the results) 5 Informing.

Now place each of the skills listed above under the most suitable heading.

Plan and perform a whole investigation to solve a problem and in the process apply the above skills.

● CURIOSITY

This is the impulse that makes you want to solve a problem, which may be related to your personal experience.

● MAKING HYPOTHESES

You create a fairly general explanation for things which occur. This leads to a prediction that can be tested. It is a good hypothesis if it is easy to test, for example, 'All dropped objects fall to the ground' is a good hypothesis: it is easy to test.

● IDENTITY, CLASSIFY, OBSERVE

You should be able to:

- **identify** things, e.g. from a written description.
- **classify** objects, e.g. on the basis of given information.
- **observe** and **describe** changes and differences in size, colour, state, etc.
- **read scales**, **measure quantities** and give good **estimates** as to their size.
- use a **consistent** set of units.

● RECORDING RESULTS

- use tables, usually.
- use them appropriately with consistent clear headings, units and order of magnitude.

● GRAPHS

1 In general:

- label axes clearly, parallel to each axis and preferably in capital letters.
- scales should be simple and clear, each filling at least half the available graph paper in each direction.
- units for each axis should be written on the graph in a consistently appropriate way, either in brackets by the axis label or after a solidus (oblique stroke). For example:

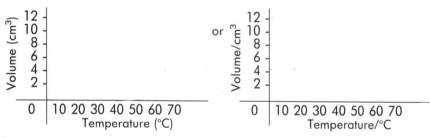

2 Line graphs:

- give your graph a title.
- decide what each axis represents.
- choose a simple scale, easy to plot and interpret information from.
- draw the best line through the points.
- only use this type of graph for variables that are continuous.

3 Bar charts:
See Chapter 13, page 117.

4 Pie charts:
See Chapter 13.

157

● DRAWING RESULTS

This is the making of general statements as a result of carrying out the investigation. A pattern should emerge from the experiment. You should also evaluate your investigation: was the plan appropriate and was the experiment a fair test? Were the results taken correctly, over the correct range, with the correct apparatus? Could the whole investigation have been improved in some way? See also Chapter 13, 'Analysis of results' and 'Conclusion'.

● DATA-ANALYSIS QUESTIONS

In many cases the need is to see how the data before you represents or requires the application of a general principle which you have studied previously. For example, you may be given data showing different rates of the loss of energy in Joules/sec. from different parts of a room (windows, outside walls, inside walls, the door, the ceiling, the floor) and you would be expected to **apply your knowledge** of energy and the units in which it is measured in order to answer questions about the total loss of energy and different rates of loss from the various parts of the room.

● 'A' LEVEL

You will need most of the GCSE skills already outlined, but to a higher degree. You must show:

1 Knowledge and recall
This should include the main facts; terminology, definitions and conventions; theories and hypotheses; techniques and equipment used in investigation; experimental methods, laws, models.

2 Comprehension
Apply known laws and principles to solve simple problems, understand and interpret scientific information presented in various forms (verbal, mathematical, graphical, etc), translate information from one form to another, recognize errors and misconceptions, make general statements about given data or scientific knowledge, use models to explain theoretical phenomena.

3 Application
Choose and apply known laws to unfamiliar problems, solve problems qualitatively and quantitatively.

4 Evaluation and investigation
Check that certain hypotheses are compatible with given information, assess observation in order to make new hypotheses or predictions, formulate methods for testing hypotheses, find the optimum solution to a problem.

5 Expression
Organize and express information and ideas clearly.

6 Practical skills
Choose and use apparatus **correctly** and safely, apply common techniques and methods, follow instructions with less (if any) help than at GCSE, describe practical situations with clear words and diagrams, make **relevant** observations and measurements with **appropriate** accuracy, look at errors, quote results to the correct order of magnitude and the correct number of decimal places or significant figures, perform calculations on measurements taken including plotting and interpreting graphs, design your own experiments, take safety precautions and explain them, recognize and correct faults and suggest improvements in the experimental arrangements, and draw valid conclusions from experimental evidence.

Index